Neurometric Evaluation of Brain Function in Normal and Learning Disabled Children

Neurometric Evaluation of Brain Function in Normal and Learning Disabled Children

E. Roy John, Ph.D.

Fellow, International Academy for Research
  in Learning Disabilities
Brain Research Laboratories
New York University Medical Center
and
L. S. Prichep, H. Ahn, H. Kaye, D. Brown,
P. Easton, B. Z. Karmel, A. Toro, R. Thatcher

**International Academy for Research in Learning
Disabilities Monograph Series, Number 5**

Ann Arbor   The University of Michigan Press

1992   1991   1990   1989   4   3   2   1

Library of Congress Cataloging-in-Publication Data

Neurometric evaluation of brain function in normal and learning
disabled children / E. Roy John . . . [et al.].
     p.   cm. —(International Academy for Research in Learning
Disabilities monograph series ; no. 5)
   Summary in French, German, and Spanish.
   Bibliography: p.
   ISBN 0-472-08085-7 (alk. paper)
   1. Learning disabilities—Physiological aspects. 2. Brain.
3. Evoked potentials (Physiology). 4. Electroencephalography.
I. John, E. Roy (Erwin Roy). II. Series.
   [DNLM: 1. Brain—physiology. 2. Electroencephalography—in
infancy & childhood. 3. Electrophysiology—in infancy & childhood.
4. Evoked Potentials—in infancy & childhood. 5. Learning
Disorders—in infancy & childhood. WL 102 N451]
RJ496.L4N47 1989
618.92′8588—dc19
DNLM/DLC
for Library of Congress   88-28076
                                                       CIP

This series of monographs published under the sponsorship of the International Academy for Research in Learning Disabilities is dedicated to the recognition of Professor Alexander Romanovich Luria, Ph.D., of the Union of Soviet Socialist Republics, a world-class professional whose work underscores a major development in an understanding of the neurophysiological development of learning disabled children and adults.

The manuscript has been read by a minimum of three members of the
Monograph Committee or by individuals not members of the Academy, but recognized as specialists in the area of the research. This
study is recognized as significant by representatives of the Academy,
but its publication by the Academy does not include International
Academy for Research in Learning Disabilities endorsement of the
research proposition, the methodology employed, or the conclusions
reached. These are the sole responsibility of the author. It is a
pleasure for the Academy to make this research available to the
academic community in the spirit of further securing solutions to the
complexities of learning disabilities.

Contents

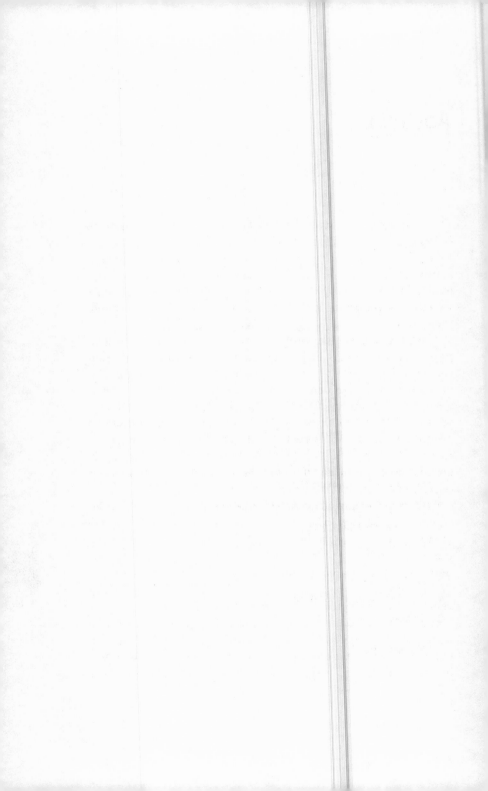

Abstract

This monograph presents the results of quantitative evaluations of the electroencephalograms (EEG) and sensory evoked potentials (EP) of large samples of normal children and children with learning disabilities (LD). The total number of children examined in this study was well over one thousand. Over fifteen years were spent collecting and analyzing these data and preparing them for publication.

On the one hand, the result is a vast compendium of electrophysiological findings describing quantitative features of brain electrical activity in normal and learning disabled children examined under an exceptionally diverse range of experimental conditions, the Neurometric Battery. On the other hand, as one surveys the differences between the normal and learning disabled groups across this wide spectrum of conditions, one cannot fail to be struck by the fact that the *differences* between these groups which are revealed by the many different test maneuvers described herein are so *similar*.

Different samples of children were studied in the different situations, and very different neurophysiological processes can plausibly be expected to be activated by each test. Nonetheless, these processes seem to be chained together into a temporal sequence of stages in the processing of information by many brain regions in parallel, and a particular subset of links in this chain appears to function differently in the LD child.

By no means does this imply that LD children constitute a homogeneous population with the same underlying pathophysiology. Rather, the dysfunctional links in different children may lie in different brain regions, and there are several links in the subset. Thus, we are led to the picture of multiple brain profiles of learning disabilities with similar behavioral features. These profiles are variations on but a few pathophysiological themes, manifested in different functional neuroanatomical systems.

The neurometric approach used in this work does not differentiate among experimental situations by verbal instructions to the child, but instead uses the testing conditions for this purpose. This reflects the preoccupation of our group with the construction of culture-fair methods of assessment and of testing methods that can be applied across the human life span, requiring no verbal comprehension or motor behaviors. The structure of each neurometric test item is intended to necessarily engage predictable processes in the normal person, and the picture of abnormality that these methods produce reveals abnormal assignments of priorities and abnormal organization of information-processing as much as it reveals pathophysiology as such. Indeed, perhaps these two aspects of brain function cannot be separately analyzed.

The items in the Neurometric Battery are divided into ten sets of tests. Set I provides estimates of structural integrity and functional maturation by quantitative analysis of EEG features. These studies yielded equations that describe the normal development of a large number of features of brain electrical activity across the age range from six to sixteen, subsequently extended from six to ninety years. Cognitively, neurologically, and psychiatrically normal individuals show few deviations from predicted values of these features, while dysfunctional patients display numerous significant deviations. The sensitivity and specificity of these developmental equations has already been confirmed in seven different countries, indicating that they describe features of brain electrical activity that are culture fair and independent of ethnic background, yet sensitive to even subtle disturbances.

Set II studies the effectiveness of photic driving at frequencies in the center of four different EEG frequency bands. This provides an index of the ease of reorganizing the transactions between different neuroanatomical systems reflected by the

EEG spectrum. Set III studies the speed of habituation of the EEG to assess how quickly a subject adjusts to a meaningless perturbation. Set IV compares EP responses to predictable versus unpredictable stimulus sequences, to assess the ability of the subject to detect and predict order in temporal relations among different sensory stimuli. Set V uses the rate of diminution of EP responses to repeated stereotypic stimulus sequences to measure the speed and amount of habituation that reflects the ability to ignore irrelevant events, the effectiveness with which novel events can achieve dishabituation that reflects adequate monitoring of the environment, and the speed of rehabituation that reflects retention of the prior experience and recognition of its return.

Using EP methods, Set VI estimates sensory acuity and effects of contrast, Set VII assesses brain mechanisms related to shape perception and size invariance, and Set VIII evaluates brain mechanisms related to letter perception. In conjunction with the information from Sets VI and VII, this permits reading disabilities such as letter reversal to be decomposed into acuity deficits, perceptual deficits, and deficits in verbal labeling of visual symbols.

Set IX assesses the subject's ability to structure figure-ground relations in a way that appropriately segregates meaningful information from noise. Set X evaluates the ability of the subject to establish learned associations between events in different sensory modalities.

These various sets of test items permit a very detailed profile to be constructed of the strengths and weaknesses (or deviations from the usual, or "normal" process) that characterize information processing in the brain of an individual child. On all of these test items, groups of LD children display significant differences from normal children. The particular items on which deviation is displayed and the particular brain regions involved vary from individual to individual, even though behavioral deficits may seem equivalent. Thus, these methods potentially offer a range of neurophysiological and neuroanatomical insights sufficiently detailed and precise to provide a basis for the development of prescriptive remedial interventions far more individualized than those based solely upon inferences drawn from analysis of behavioral capabilities as reflected in neuropsychological assessments. Hopefully, workers in special education will find this monograph useful for that purpose.

Abstrakt

Dieser Artikel legt die Ergebnisse von den Elektroenzephalo-
grammen (EEG) und von durch die Sinne hervorgerufenen Po-
tentialen vor, die durch große Proben von normalen bzw.
von geistesbehinderten Kindern gewonnen wurden. Die Gesamt-
zahl von Kindern, die in dieser Studie geprüft wurden, belief
sich auf über eintausend. Uber 15 Jahre wurden damit ver-
bracht, diese Daten zu sammeln, zu analysieren und sie zur
Veröffentlichung vorzubereiten.

Die Ergebnisse sind einerseits eine große Sammlung von
elektrophysiologischen Entdeckungen, die quantitative Merkmale der elektrischen Gehirntätigkeiten in normalen bzw.
geistesbehinderten Kindern beschreiben, die unter äußerst di-
versen Bedingungen (d.h. "Neurometric Battery") geprüft
wurden. Wenn man sich aber andererseits die Unterschiede
zwischen den normalen Kindern und den behinderten Gruppen
genauer ansieht, fällt es sofort auf, daß die Unterschiede, die
durch die im folgenden beschriebenen Prüfverfahren klarge-
macht werden, eigentlich gleichartig sind.

Verschiedene Proben von Kindern in verschiedenen Situationen wurden erforscht, und man durfte natürlich damit rech-
nen, daß jede Probe sehr verschiedenartige neurophysio-
logische Vorgänge aktivierte. Während der Verarbeitung von
Informationen durch viele Gehirnteile scheinen sich aber diese
Vorgänge in einer zeitlichen Folge von Stadien parallel mitein-
ander verkettet zu haben. Und eine besondere Untergruppe
von Gliedern in dieser Kette scheinen in dem geistesbehinderten Kind anders zu funktionieren.

Auf keinen Fall soll das heißen, daß geistesbehinderte

Kinder eine homogene Gruppe mit derselben zugrunde-
liegenden Pathophysiologie bilden. Es ist vielmehr der Fall, daß
die in verschiedenen Kindern sich befindlichen nicht funktion-
ierenden Kettenglieder in verschiedenen Gehirnteilen liegen
dürfen, und es gibt mehrere Kettenglieder in der Untergruppe.
Daher gelangen wir zu einem Gesamtbild mit mehreren Gehirn-
beschreibungen mit ähnlichen Verhaltensweisen. Diese Beschreibungen stellen Abweichungen von eigentlich ganz wen-
igen pathophysiologischen Grundthemen dar, die sich in verschiedenen funktionellen neuroantomischen Systemen zeigen.

Die neurometrische Methode, die in dieser Arbeit verwendet
wurde, unterscheidet nicht unter experimentellen Situationen
durch mündliche Anweisungen, die dem Kind gegeben werden,
sondern diese Methode gebraucht die Prüfbedingungen zu
diesem Zweck. Das spiegelt sich in der Sorgfalt unserer
Gruppe, kulturgerechte Bewertungen zu konstruieren und in
den Prüfverfahren, deren Anwendungsbereich das ganze Leben
erfaßt und die kein Hörverständnis und keine motorischen
Fähigkeiten fordern. Der Aufbau von jedem Testpunkt soll
notwendigerweise darauf gezielt sein, voraussagbare Vorgänge
im normalen Menschen hervorzurufen, und die Abnormität, die
diese Methoden ermitteln, zeigt sowohl eine abnormale Fest-
setzung von Prioritäten und eine abnormale Gestaltung der
Verarbeitung von Informationen, als auch die Pathophysiologie. In der Tat werden sich wohl diese zwei Aspekte der
Hirnfunktion nicht getrennt analysieren lassen.

Die Punkte in der "Neurometric Battery" sind in zehn
Testgruppen eingeteilt. Gruppe I verschafft durch eine quantitative Analyse der Merkmale der Elektroenzephalogramme
Bewertungen der Konstruktionsintegrität und der Funktions-
reife. Diese Studien ergaben Gleichungen, die die normale
Entwicklung einer großen Anzahl von Merkmalen der elektrischen Gehirntätigkeit zwischen sechs und sechszehn Jahren
(später zwischen sechs und neunzig Jahren) beschreiben.
Menschen, die kognitiv, neurologisch und psychiatrisch normal
sind, zeigen wenige Abweichungen von den vorausgesagten

Werten dieser Merkmale, während lernbehinderte Patienten
zahlreiche bedeutsame Abweichungen zeigen. Die Sensitivität
und die Spezifizität dieser Entwicklungsgleichungen sind in
sieben verschiedenen Ländern schon bestätigt worden, was
andeutet, daß sie Merkmale der elektrischen Gehirntätigkeit
beschreiben, die kulturgerecht und unabhängig von ethnischen
Lebensumständen und auch gegen subtile Störungen empfind-
lich sind.

Gruppe II erforscht die Wirksamkeit der photischen Kraft in
der Mitte von vier verschiedenen EEG-Frequenzbändern, was
uns mit einem Index versieht, der die Leichtigkeit der
Neuordnung der Ubergänge zwischen verschiedenen neuroanatomischen Systemen beschreiben, die sich in dem EEG-
Spektrum spiegeln. Gruppe III erforscht die Schnelligkeit des
Anpassungsvermögens der EEG, um einzuschätzen, wie schnell
ein Patient sich einer bedeutungslosen Störung anpaßt. Gruppe
IV vergleicht EP-Reaktionen auf voraussagbare bzw. unvor-
aussagbare Stimulus-Folgen, um die Fähigkeit des Patienten,
die Ordnung der zeitlichen Beziehungen von verschiedenen
Stimuli festzustellen und vorauszusagen, zu beurteilen. Gruppe
V verwendet die Verminderungsrate der EG-Reaktionen auf
wiederholte stereotypische Stimulus-Folgen, um die Schnelligkeit und die Quantität der Habituierung zu messen, was die
Fähigkeit zeigt, unwichtige Ereignisse zu ignorieren, mit deren
Wirksamkeit neue Ereignisse, in der Dishabituierung erreicht
werden können, wasa zweierlei zeigt—ausreichendes Moniter-
ing der Umgebung und die Schnelligkeit der Neuhabituierung,
die das Festhalten der früheren Erfahrung und die Anerken-
nung deren Wiederkehr widerspiegelt.

Durch EP-Methoden schätzt Gruppe VI Sinneswahrneh-
mungen und Kontrastwirkungen ein; Gruppe VII bewertet
Hirnmechanismen, die mit Formerkenntnis und Größenbeständ-
igkeit verbunden sind; und Gruppe VIII beurteilt Gehirn-
mechanismen, die mit Buchstabenerkenntnis verbunden sind.
Im Zusammenhang mit den Informationen von Gruppen VI
und VII ist es möglich, Leseschwierigkeiten (wie z.B. Buch-

stabenumkehrung) in Schärfe-Defizite, Erkenntnis-Defizite und Defizite in der Benennung von sichtbaren Gegenständen aufzulösen.

Gruppe IX bewertet die Fähigkeit des Patienten, auf Gestalt beruhende Beziehungen auf eine Art aufzubauen, die bedeutungsvolle Informationen von Geräusch trennt. Gruppe X beurteilt die Fähigkeit des Patienten, erlernte Beziehungen zwischen Ereignissen in verschiedenen Sinnesmodalitäten festzustellen.

Durch diese Gruppen von Testpunkten läßt sich ein sehr detailliertes Bild der Stärken und Schwächen (oder der Abweichungen vom gewöhnlichen bzw. "normalen" Prozeß) malen, das die Verarbeitung von Informationen im Gehirn eines einzelnen Kindes kennzeichnet. Bei all diesen Testpunkten zeigen die Gruppen von lernbehinderten Kindern beträchtliche Abweichungen von normalen Kindern. Die einzelnen Punkte, durch die sich eine Abweichung zeigt, und die daran beteiligten spezifischen Gehirnteile sind von Individuum zu Individuum verschieden, obwohl Verhaltensdefizite gleichwertig erscheinen dürfen. Daher bieten diese Methoden eine Reihe von neurophysiologischen bzw. neuroanatomischen Einsichten an, die dermaßen detailliert und präzise sind, daß eine Basis für die Entwicklung von präskriptiven Heilmethoden gebildet werden kann, die das Individuum mehr in Betracht zieht als die Methoden, die ausschließlich auf Schlüssen beruhen, die aus der Beurteilung von Verhaltenskapazitäten gezogen werden, die sich in neurophysiological Bewertungen sehen lassen. Hoffentlich können zu diesem Zweck die Arbeitskräfte in der Erziehungswissenschaft Gebrauch von diesem Artikel machen.

Résumé

Ce monographe présente les résultats de l'évaluation quantitative d'éléctroencephalogrammes (EEG) et de potentiels évoques (PE) sensoriels de groupes importants d'enfants normaux et d'enfants avec difficultés de comprehension (DC). Le nombre total d'enfants examinés par cette étude depasse un millier. Plus de quinze ans fûrent investis à amasser et analyser ces données et en les préparant a être publiés.

D'une part, le resultat est une compilation de conclusions éléctrophysiologiques qui décrivent les caracteristiques quantitiatives de l'activité éléctrique cérébrale d'enfants normaux et avec difficultés de comprehension, examinés sous un régime exceptionellement varié de conditions experimentales, la "Batterie de Tests Neurométriques". D'autre part, en examinant les differences entre les groupes normaux et avec DC à travers ce spectre ample de conditions, l'on ne peut s'empècher de remarquer que les differences entre ces groupes qui sont révèles par les differentes manœuvres décrites sont tellement semblables.

Differents échantillons d'enfants fûrent étudies sous differentes conditions, et il est probable que chaque test entraine l'activation de differents procésus neurophysiologiques. Tout de même, ces procésus semblent s'enchainer, formant une séquence temporelle d'étapes de l'interpretation d'information par nombreuses regions cérébrales en parallèle, et un sous-ensemble particulier de procesus consecutifs paraît fonctionner diferemment dans l'enfant DC.

Ceci ne veut pas dire que les enfants avec DC constituent une population homogene, avec une pathologie subjacente commune. Plutôt, les sousensembles disfonctionels de la sequence correspondent probablement à differentes regions cérébrales, et chaque sousensemble comprend plusieurs procésus. Nous sommes donc menés a l'image de profils cérébraux multiples de difficultes de comprehension, avec des caracteristiques de conduite semblables. Ces profils sont des variations d'un petit ensemble de physiopathologies, qui se manifestent dans differents systèmes fonctionels neuroanatomiques.

L'approche neurométrique utilisée dans cette étude ne differentie pas parmi situations experimentales a partir d'instructions verbales données a l'enfant, mais utilise plutôt les conditions du test eux-memes à cet effet. Ceci reflette la préoccupation de notre groupe avec la construction de methodes d'évaluation qui sont independantes d'age et de culture, et qui ne necessitent aucune comprehension verbale ou activitée moteur. La structure de chaque composante d'une étude neurométrique a pour objectif d'engager nécessairement des procésus prévisibles dans une personne normale, et l'image d'abnormalité que produisent ces methodes révèle un assignmement anormal des priorités et une organisation anormale des procésus d'interpretation d'information autant qu'elles révèlent la physiopathologie elle-même. Il se peut que ces deux aspects de la fonction cérébrale ne peuvent être analysés séparément.

La Batterie de Tests Neurométriques est composée de dix ensembles d'épreuves. Le premier ensemble permet d'éstimer l'integrité structurale et la maturation fonctionelle en analyzant de façon quantitative les caracteristiques de l'EEG. A partir de ces études, l'on a obtenu des équations décrivant le developement normal d'un nombre important de caracteristiques de l'activité cérébrale dans la gamme d'ages de six à seize ans, par apres étendu à six à 90 ans. Les personnes présentant un profil cognitif, neurologique et psychiatrique normal dévient très peu des valeurs prédites. Par contre, les patients disfoncionels démontrent nombreuses déviations significatives. La sensibilité et la specificité des ces équations developmentales a deja été confirmée das sept pais differents, indiquant qu'elles decrivent des caracteristiques de l'activité cérébrale indépendantes de milieu culturel ou d'origine éthnique, et qui cependant sont sensibles au déviations subtiles.

Le deuxieme ensemble étudie l'effet de stimulation visuelle à quatre frequences correspondant aux centres des bandes de frequence de l'EEG. Ceci donne un indice de la facilité à la réorganization des transactions entre differents systèmes que reflette le spèctre d'EEG. L'ensemble III étudie la vitesse d'habituation de l'EEG afin de déterminer la vitesse avec laquelle le sujet se réajuste à la suite d'une perturbation qui n'a aucun sens en soi. L'ensemble IV compare les réponses de PE aux séquences de stimulus à intervale prévisible par raport à celles à intervale imprévisible, afin de mesurer l'abilité du sujet de détécter et prévoir l'ordre temporel de stimulus sensoriels variés. L'ensemble V utilise la rapidité de diminution des réponses de PE aux stimulus stéreotypiques répétes pour mesurer la vitesse d'habituation, qui reflette l'abilité d'ignorer les evènements extranés, l'éfféctivite avec laquelle un nouvel évènement provoque une deshabituation, qui réflette une attention adequate prétée a l'environnement, et la vitesse de rehabituation, qui réflette la retention de l'experience anterieure et la reconaissance de son retour.

Utilisant des methodes de PE, l'ensemble VI éstime l'activité sensorielle et les éffets de contraste, l'ensemble VII évalue les mechanismes cérébraux qui permettent la percéption de formes et d'invariance de grandeur, et l'ensemble VIII évalue les mechanismes cérébraux qui permettent la percéption des lettres. En conjonction avec l'information des ensembles VI et VII, ceci permet les difficultes de lecture (telles que l'inversion des lettres) d'etre decomposées en déficits d'acuité, déficits perceptuels, ou déficits de la classification verbale de symboles visuels.

L'ensemble IX évalue l'abilité d'un sujet a structurer les relations figure-fond de façon a séparer adéquatement l'information du bruit. L'ensemble X evalue l'abilité du sujet a établir des associations apprises entre des evenements associés a des modalités sensorielles differentes.

Ces ensembles variés de tests permettent de construire un profil très detaillé des aspects positifs et negatifs (ou deviations du proçes "normal") qui caracterisent le procésus d'interpretation d'information dans le cerveau d'un enfant individuel. Pour tous ces tests, les groupes d'enfants avec DC démontrent des differences importantes de groupes d'enfants normaux. Les caracteristiques particulières où l'on encontre la déviation et les regions cérébrales impliquées varient d'un individu a l'autre, quoique les déficits de conduite peuvent paraître semblables. Donc, ces methodes offrent une gamme d'information neuro-physiologique et neuroanatomique suffisemment détaillée et précise pour servir de base pour le developement d'interventions rémédiales beaucoup plus individualisés que celles basées entièrement sur les conclusions qui resultent de l'analyse des capabilités de conduite qui parviennent d'un examen neurologique. Nous souhaitons que ce monographe paraîtra a ce effet util a ceux qui travaillent dans les écoles d'éducation spéciale.

Sumario

Esta monografia presenta los resultados de las evaluaciones cuantitativas de los electroencefalogramas (EEG) y de los potenciales evocados (PE) sensoriales de muestras grandes de niños normales y niños con trastornos del aprendizaje (TA). La cantidad total de niños examinados en este estudio es superior al millar. Más de 15 años fueron invertidos en la recolección y el análisis de los datos y en la preparación de su publicación. Por una parte, se presenta una extensa recopilación de resultados electrofisiológicos que describen los características cuantitativas de la actividad eléctrica cerebral en niños normales y con trastornos del aprendizaje, examinados bajo un rango excepcionalmente amplio de condiciones experimentales, la "Batería de Pruebas Neurométricas". Por otra parte, a medida que se inspeccionan las diferencias entre los grupos normales y con trastornos del aprendizaje a través de este amplio espectro de condiciones, uno no puede dejar de sorprenderse por el hecho de que las *diferencias* entre estos grupos, las cuales se manifiestan mediante diversas maniobras descritas en este trabajo, sean tan *similares*.

Diferentes muestras de niños fueron estudiadas en diferentes condiciones, y es probable que se hayan activado procesos neurofisiológicos diferentes en cada condicion. Sin embargo, estos procesos parecen estar concatenados en forma de una secuencia temporal de distintas etapas en el procesamiento de la información, debido a muchas regiones cerebrales en paralelo. En el caso del niño con TA, parece que un subconjunto particular de las etapas en el proceso concatenado funciona de forma diferente.

Esto no quiere decir que los niños con TA constituyan una población homogénea con una fisiopatología subyacente común, sino mas bien que las etapas con disfunción del proceso concatenado probablemente correspondan a diferentes regiones cerebrales, y que existen varias etapas en el subconjunto. De aquí que emerge el cuadro de múltiples perfiles cerebrales de trastornos del aprendizaje con características conductuales similares. Estos perfiles son variaciones de un pequeño conjunto de fisiopatologías, las cuales se manifiestan en sistemas neuroanatómicos funcionalmente diferentes.

El enfoque neurométrico utilizado en este trabajo no distingue entre situaciones experimentales basadas en instrucciones verbales dadas al niño, sino en el uso de las condiciones de pruebas para este propósito. Esto refleja la preocupación de nuestro grupo por el desarrollo de métodos de medición y de estudio que sean independientes de la cultura, los cuales puedan ser aplicados para cualquier edad, y que no requieran de entendimiento verbal ni de conducta motora. La estructura de cada componente de prueba neurométrica tiene como objetivo involucrar de forma necesaria procesos predictibles en la persona normal, con lo cual se produce un cuadro de anormalidad donde se manifiestan asignaciones anormales de prioridad y organización anormal del procesamiento de la información, relacionadas a la fisiopatología. Es muy posible que no puedan analizarse por separado estos dos aspectos de la función cerebral.

La Batería Neurométrica se divide en 10 Conjuntos de pruebas. El Conjunto I brinda estimadores de la integridad estructural y de la maduración funcional mediante el análisis cuantitativo de las características del EEG. A partir de estos estudios se obtuvieron ecuaciones que describen el desarrollo normal de una gran cantidad de características de la actividad eléctrica en el rango de edades entre 6 y 16 años, extendiéndose posteriormente hasta los 90 años. Los sujetos normales (normalidad con respecto a los aspectos cognitivos, neurológicos y siquíatricos) muestran pocas desviaciones de los valores esperados de las medidas, mientras que los pacientes con disfunciones presentan una gran cantidad de desviaciones significativas. La sensitividad y especificidad de estas ecuaciones del desarrollo han sido confirmadas ya en siete países diferentes, lo cual indica que ellas describen características de la actividad eléctrica cerebral que son independientes del desarrollo cultural y del orígen étnico, y que sin embargo son sensitivas a desviaciones más sutiles.

El Conjunto II estudia el efecto del seguimiento a la estimulación visual a frecuencias correspondientes a los centros de las cuatro bandas de frecuencia del EEG. Esto brinda un índice de la facilidad para la reorganización de las transiciones entre diferentes sistemas neuroanatómicos, relacionado al espectro de potencia del EEG. El Conjunto III estudia la velocidad de habituamiento del EEG como una medida de cuán rápidamente un sujeto se reajusta a perturbaciones carentes de sentido. El Conjunto IV compara las respuestas evocadas ante secuencias de estímulos predictibles e impredictibles, con el objetivo de evaluar la habilidad del sujeto en la deteccíon y predicción de orden en relaciones temporales entre estimulaciones sensoriales diferentes. El Conjunto V se basa en la disminución de las respuestas evocadas ante secuencias de estímulos estereotípicos repetidos, para medir la velocidad y la magnitud del habituamiento relacionada a la habilidad de ignorar eventos irrelevantes; la efectividad con la cual un nuevo evento puede lograr el deshabituamiento, lo cual refleja un adecuado monitoreo del entorno; y la velocidad de rehabituamiento, la cual refleja la retención de la experiencia previa y el reconocimiento de su repetición.

Mediante el uso de los PEs, el Conjunto VI estima la agudeza sensorial y los efectos de contraste, el Conjunto VII evalúa los mecanismos cerebrales relacionados a la percepción de forma y de invarianza de tamaño, y el Conjunto VIII evalúa los mecanismos cerebrales relacionados a la percepción de letras. En conjunción con la información de los Conjuntos VI y VII, esto permite descomponer los trastornos de la lectura (tal como la inversión de letras) en defectos de la agudeza, defectos perceptuales y en defectos de la clasificación verbal de símbolos visuales.

El Conjunto IX evalúa la habilidad del sujeto para estructurar las relaciones figura-fondo de manera que queden separada adecuadamente la información del ruido. El Conjunto X evalúa la habilidad del sujeto para el establecimiento de asociaciones ya aprendidas entre eventos bajo modalidades sensoriales diferentes.

Estos conjuntos diferentes de pruebas neurométricas permiten la construcción de perfiles muy detallados de los aspectos fuertes y débiles (o las desviaciones del proceso usual o "normal") que caracterizan el procesamiento de información en el cerebro de un niño individual. En todas estas pruebas, los grupos de niños con TA muestran diferencias significativas con respecto a los niños normales. Las medidas particulares en las que se manifiestan desviaciones y las regiones cerebrales particulares involucradas varían de individuo a individuo, aunque los defectos conductuales puedan parecer equivalentes. De aquí que estos métodos brinden potencialmente un amplio rango de información neurofisiológica y neuroanatómica lo suficientemente detallada y precisa que sirva de base para el desarrollo de intervenciones remediales prescriptivas mucho más individualizadas que aquellas basadas solamente en las conclusiones derivadas del análisis de la capacidad conductual relacionadas a las evaluaciones neurosicológicas. Es nuestro deseo que esta monografía sea de utilidad a los que trabajan en escuelas de educación especial.

CHAPTER 1

Introduction

This monograph is based upon a large-scale project on quantitative evaluation of brain functions, as reflected in the electroencephalograph (EEG) and evoked potentials (EP) recorded from normal and learning disabled children. These electrophysiological data were collected under a wide range of carefully specified test conditions called the Neurometric Battery. The Neurometric Battery was devised to provide information about the anatomical integrity of the nervous system and about the processes mediating a wide variety of sensory, perceptual, and cognitive functions.

The project began in 1973, with funding from the Research Applied to National Needs (RANN) Program of the National Science Foundation (Grant Nos. DAR 78-18772 and APR 76-24662). Data collection continued until 1979, with NSF support augmented by grants from the Bureau for the Educationally Handicapped of the U.S. Office of Education (Grant No. G008704516). In 1979, support for this project terminated abruptly. At that point, data had been collected from 398 male and 238 female normally functioning children from five to sixteen years of age and from 905 male and 208 female children with specific or generalized learning disabilities, from five to twenty-one years of age.

The amount of effort and expenditure of funds involved in collecting this volume of data was great. The withdrawal of government funding occurred after this massive data bank had been collected but while the bulk of it was yet unanalyzed. Since the information in the data bank spanned a unique space and was potentially of substantial practical value, we were faced with the responsibility of completing its analysis. In the intervening years, we have utilized resources of the Brain Research Laboratories as they became available to analyze those data and to prepare this monograph.

We focused our initial attention on the analysis of the EEG data because it represented a relatively small, discrete portion of the Neurometric Battery. Several articles have already been published describing our EEG findings. These results will be summarized in the appropriate section of this monograph but are not presented in full detail since they are readily available. The major emphasis of this monograph is upon the evoked potential methods and findings that are the bulk of the data yet unreported.

The purpose of this monograph is primarily to present these findings. It is beyond the scope of this volume to attempt a comprehensive review of all electrophysiological research on learning disability that has been published in this decade. Other workers have undertaken that task. *The bulk of the literature cited herein is that which provided the bases and rationale for the design of the Neurometric Battery, rather than later contributions.* However, our computer searches of the relevant literature from 1979 until 1987 uncovered a remarkably small amount of research on this topic. This indicates that the withdrawal of federal support from this vital field of inquiry has had a devastating impact. It is deplorable that this neglect occurred just when a number of promising new methods had appeared that provide the opportunity to make major advances in early detection and remediation of the learning disabled child. Unfortunately, children have a far less vocal constituency than armaments.

This monograph begins with a review of the electrophysiological literature that provided the factual and conceptual bases for construction of the Neurometric Battery (NB) and for selection of the stimulus conditions that constitute the successive test items. A discussion of the basic strategy that underlies the NB concludes the introduction.

Chapter 3 describes all procedures in sufficient detail to permit replication of any aspect of this work, and includes: the source and selection criteria for both normal (N) and learning disabled (LD) subjects, the recording procedures, the amplifiers and data acquisition system, the artifacting algorithm used for on-line quality control, the on-line computation of average evoked potentials and variances, and digital storage of all data. See appendix 1 for the specifications and intent of each item in the NB. Chapter 3 continues with a description of visual editing for further quality control prior to quantitative analysis and describes the hardware and software of the data analysis system. Our EEG analysis methods are reviewed, with descriptions and discussions of the digital filtering approach used for spectral analysis, the advantages of converting from absolute to relative power measures, the derivation of polynomial functions specifying the changes in normative data about EEG spectral features in each brain region as a function of age, the computation of coherence and power asymmetry measures, and the rationale for Z transform of all EEG descriptors. The chapter then proceeds to a discussion of the techniques used for EP analysis. Computation of averages and variances are briefly described, followed by definitions of a series of quantitative descriptors of various features of the EP, including signal strength, signal-to-noise ratio, signal asymmetry between homologous pairs of leads, the signal-to-noise ratio of asymmetries, and a new quantitative descriptor of waveshape morphology that we have devised. The generation of normative data for the full 10/20 system for each of these quantitative descriptors of the EP, in each of several latency bands, is then reviewed and the Z-transform procedure for EP features is discussed, as well as the hit matrix that permits concise presentation of such data.

The results are presented in chapters 4, 5, and 6. Chapter 4 is intended to permit the reader to evaluate the adequacy of the methods that have been utilized in this work. The feasibility of administering the NB to LD as well as normal children is first examined. The validity of the automatic artifact rejection algorithm and test-retest reliability is then assessed, utilizing quantitative EEG data. The results indicate that the electrophysiological measures obtained using the neurometric methods are a reliable characteristic of the individual. Coefficients are presented for the family of sixteen fourth-order polynomials that describe the evolution of spectral features in each brain region as a function of age. The accuracy of prediction of EEG features by these regression equations is evaluated in great detail. The distribution of Z-transformed values of spectral estimators in each brain region is presented for a variety of different samples of normal children. The incidence of false positive values in each of these groups was found to be at or below the chance level for most variables. No significant differences from the distributions predicted by the normative polynomials were found for any of these groups. Further, no significant differences were found between groups of normal healthy children from urban, suburban, or rural settings in the United States and in Barbados; between groups of children from different ethnic backgrounds; or between groups of male and female children.

In chapter 5, results are presented that show that the distribution of the EEG spectral estimators in different groups of LD children was significantly different from the distribution in an independent group of normal children. These findings provide a replicated demonstration that the EEG spectral estimates predicted by the polynomial functions are not only stable, replicable, and unbiased measures of brain electrical activity in normal children, but reflect aspects of brain function that are altered in a high proportion of children with learning disabilities. Further results obtained from international collaborative studies (chap. 6) provide additional confirmation that these spectral estimators are the same in healthy children from different cultures and are sensitive to processes that are often altered in children with cognitive dysfunctions.

Chapter 7 presents our findings with the EP measures of the NB. First of all, Grand Average EPs were computed for groups of normal and learning disabled children from every lead of the

10/20 system for every one of the approximately eighty EP conditions and challenges of the NB. Difference waveshapes between normal and learning disabled Grand Average EPs were computed for each lead and test item, and the significance of the intergroup differences assessed by the t-test at 10 millisecond latency intervals. It is important to bear in mind, as one evaluates these findings, that the *actual individuals* comprising N and LD samples differed from test item to test item, since most children were only tested on some subset of NB items. This fact makes it all the more striking that significant intergroup differences were consistently found within certain restricted latency intervals in particular leads, even though the specific stimulation conditions varied very markedly from item to item.

These findings are presented as a latency histogram of significant intergroup differences by lead across items. They indicate that in spite of the undoubted heterogeneity of both the N and LD groups, a substantial proportion of each LD group displayed a characteristic dysfunction in information processing mechanisms at particular latencies, no matter what the explicit content of the information being processed. Although enormous numbers of t-tests were computed in these comparisons, the consistency of the latency intervals in which significant intergroup differences appeared make it highly implausible that these findings can be attributed to chance.

Using a multivariate measure of waveshape morphology, the Mahalanobis distance across latencies, a measure of intergroup differences in EP waveshape was devised that was completely independent of the tests of group Grand Average differences just described (chap. 8). Results with the two types of measure were compared and showed good agreement for a large number of leads and test items. Distributions of this morphology measure were determined for substantial groups of normal and LD children for every 10/20 lead and test item. It was shown that significant discrimination between children in the N and LD groups could be accomplished, using the Mahalanobis distance measure to quantify the extent to which an individual EP deviated from the distribution of waveshape morphologies observed in independent samples of normal children.

Next, normative data were gathered for a set of quantitative descriptors of distinct features of the EP from every 10/20 lead and NB test item (chap. 9). The distributions of these normative data were examined and found to be Gaussian in most cases, or were transformed to achieve such distributions. In independent replicated samples of normal and LD children, the distributions of these EP descriptors were compared. Many significant intergroup differences were found and are tallied for each 10/20 lead and NB item.

Finally, a preliminary stepwise linear discriminant function was computed for groups of normal, specifically learning disabled, and generally learning disabled children, separately for EEG and EP features and for the two types of data combined. These discriminant functions were jack-knife replicated. These results showed that these measures permit classification of normal and LD children at a level high enough to be of practical utility and of reasonable replicability. Since these later studies were carried out on subgroups of children using only a limited fraction of the available data, we consider them as pilot studies.

We wish to acknowledge the assistance of Nina Brennan, Monique Granville, Lillian Lebron, and Michaela Lobel in the preparation of this manuscript, and the invaluable editorial assistance and literature review provided by Dr. Robert Chabot.

CHAPTER 2

Early Electrophysiological Studies: The Background of the Neurometric Battery

Childhood can be a period of frustration and alienation for the many children who have difficulties in school. For a number of these children, learning disabilities are due to deviations from normal brain function. Estimates of the prevalence of learning disability due to brain dysfunction vary from 1 percent to 15 percent of the school-age population (Eisenberg 1966; HEW 1969; Minskoff 1973; Myklebust and Boshes 1969; Silverman and Metz 1973; Wender 1971). Based on these estimates at least two million school children in the United States, and perhaps as many as ten million are limited in their learning by some form of brain dysfunction. Some have considered the diagnosis and treatment of brain dysfunction in learning disabled children among the most urgent problems facing neurologists.

These learning disabilities cost an undoubtedly staggering price in both human and economic terms. Failure to recognize and treat learning disability leads to increased tensions with the family, peer groups, and educators, and results in increased risk for psychopathology later in life, ranging from poor social adjustment, underachievement, and scholastic failure, to juvenile delinquency and even psychosis (Gittelman et al. 1985; Hechtman, Weiss, and Perlman 1984; Kirk 1972; Menkes, Rowe, and Menkes 1967; Satterfield, Hoppe, and Schell 1982; Weiss and Minde 1974; Weiss et al. 1971).

Learning disabled children do not display invariant neurological or behavioral signs but may show one or several of a

7

wide variety of characteristics, some of which are also displayed by children without brain dysfunctions (Conners 1971, 1973; Rouke 1985; Wender 1971). It is obvious that many different causes may underly failure to achieve an expected behavioral or psychometric performance; the dysfunctional process in any particular case cannot be inferred by examining the deficient product. Thus, a crucial element in the attempt to aid a child with learning difficulties is the ability to establish unequivocally the presence or absence of brain dysfunctions and, if present, to specify the anatomical location and functional manifestations of the disorder as completely as possible. Most workers in the field admit inability to make differential diagnosis and recognize that learning disabled children are a heterogeneous population (Clark 1968; Gallagher 1973; Keogh 1971; Rouke 1985; Satz, Morris, and Fletcher 1985; Shucard et al. 1985).

A review of the literature reveals abundant evidence establishing that, in general, the electroencephalogram (EEG) and sensory average evoked responses or event-related potentials (EP or ERP) can be used to assess the anatomical integrity, functional status, and maturational development of the brain, and to evaluate information processing related to sensory, perceptual, and cognitive functions. Numerous detailed reviews of this evidence are available (Callaway, Tueting, and Koslow 1978; Cracco and Bodis-Wollner 1986; Desmedt 1977; John 1977; Otto 1978; Regan 1972; Shagass 1977). Most of these assessment goals are extremely difficult or impossible to achieve by conventional neurological or psychometric methods. Electrophysiological observations offer the unique way in which these processes can be directly assessed.

To date, clinical application of electrophysiological methods to evaluation of learning disabled children or patients with neurological diseases has been greatly limited by the qualitative way in which the results were analyzed, requiring visual inspection of EEG or EP waveshapes by skilled and experienced personnel. With the advent of economical and powerful minicomputers, many investigators have turned their attention to the problem of quantitative analysis of electrophysiological data, devising methods to extract clinically useful features in numerical forms that would be amenable to objective statistical analysis (Dolce and Kimble 1975; John, Ruchkin, and Vidal 1978; John, Prichep, and Easton 1987; Kellaway and Petersen 1973; Remonde 1972).

In specific, much evidence exists that available electrophysiological measurements reflect brain functions that are often abnormal in learning disabled children. The electrophysiological phenomena that seem particularly well suited to explore for abnormality in certain brain functions, which seem likely to be critically important for a child to learn efficiently, are reviewed below.

EEG Spectral Analysis

Limited normative baselines for the absolute power of different frequency bands of the EEG from various regions of the scalp, from birth to maturity, were published in 1973 (Hagne et al. 1973; Matousek and Petersen 1973). These norms reveal a systematic evolution of the EEG with maturation and therefore permit objective evaluation of whether or not a particular child shows a maturational deviation in the spectral composition of his or her EEG in different regions. In general, with maturation there is a steady decrease in the amount of slow waves in each region. Many studies have revealed a high incidence of abnormal EEG activity in children who were underachievers, or who had speech problems, reading disorders, dyslexia, or other learning or behavioral difficulties, although the neurological examination of such children was usually within normal limits, and their intelligence was average (Ahn et al. 1980; Benton and Bird 1963; Capute, Niedermeyer, and Richardson 1968; Cohn and Nardini 1958; Colon et al. 1979; Duffy and Geschwind 1985; Gasser et al. 1983; Gergen et al. 1965; Hughes 1968, 1985; Hughes and Mykelbust 1966; Hughes and Park 1966; John et al. 1983; Klove 1959; Leisman and Ashkenazi 1980; Lubar et al.

1985; Muehl, Knott, and Benton 1965; Pavy and Metcalfe 1965; Prichep et al. 1983; Ritvo et al. 1970; Ryers 1967; Satterfield 1973; Sklar, Hanley, and Simmons 1972, 1973; Sokal and Sneath 1963; Stevens, Sachev, and Milstein 1968; Torres and Ayers 1968; Wikler, Dixon, and Parker 1970). Hughes noted a 45 percent incidence of EEG abnormality in dyslexia as an over-all mean for ten studies involving 530 patients (Hughes 1968, 1985).

Excessive slow wave activity is seen with high incidence (14 percent) in unselected referrals, and has often been reported to be commonly associated with behavioral learning difficulties. Many of the workers cited above have asserted that the most common EEG abnormality found in learning disabled or hyperactive children is excessive slow waves. One might conclude that excessive slow wave activity represents a maturational lag in brain development of a substantial subgroup of learning disabled children, as has been proposed by Kinsbourne (1973). This suggested that a quantitative definition of the amount of slow waves in excess of the proportion expected in a particular brain region, as a function of the age of a child, could reasonably be expected to reveal abnormalities in many children with learning disabilities. Accordingly, we constructed norms for four broad spectral bands (delta, theta, alpha, and beta) in both monopolar and bipolar derivations.

EEG Symmetry Analysis

Electroencephalographers are in general agreement that the EEG recorded from bilaterally symmetrical, or *homologous,* regions of the scalp in normal healthy persons is extremely symmetrical with respect both to amplitude and waveshape, whether analyzed qualitatively (Gibbs and Gibbs 1950) or quantitatively (Harmony et al. 1973; Matousek and Petersen 1973). At the same time, some investigators have reported a high incidence of asymmetry in the resting EEG of dyslexic children or underachievers (Duffy et al. 1980; Duffy and

McAnulty 1985; Gergen et al. 1965; Leisman and Ashkenazi 1980; Lubar and Deering 1981; Muehl, Knott, and Benton 1965) and in a variety of neurological dysfunctions (Harmony, 1983; Otero, Harmony, and Ricardo 1975a, b). These observations directed our attention to the possible utility of quantitative measures of EEG and EP power symmetry for the detection of brain dysfunctions among a subgroup of learning disabled children. It seemed likely that measures of coherence between homologous leads might also be useful, since they provide a precise way to estimate waveshape synchronization.

EPs in Learning Disabled Children

Children with learning disabilities often show EPs that are poorly formed (lack components), show long latency, are unusually asymmetrical, are exceptionally variable, or show anomalous regional differentiation (Barnet and Lodge 1967; Bigum, Dustman, and Beck 1970; Buchsbaum and Wender 1973; Cohen and Breslin 1984; Conners 1971; Duffy and McAnulty 1985; Lelord et al. 1973; Rhodes, Dustman, and Beck 1969; Sutton et al. 1986). Some reports assert that particular component amplitudes are smaller than normal in learning disabled children (Cohen 1980; Cohen and Breslin 1984; Loiselle et al. 1980; Lovrich and Stamm 1983; Ollo and Squires 1986; Otto et al. 1984; Preston, Guthrie, and Childs 1974; Prichep, Sutton, and Hakerem 1976; Satterfield 1973; Sobotka and May 1977.

These findings suggested several desirable features of recording and data analysis procedures that could be identified, no matter what stimuli or conditions were used to evaluate EPs in learning disabled children. These included the need to record from a broad region of the scalp so responses of different regions can be compared under various conditions, the necessity to measure variability of responses routinely, and the need for quantitative measures of EP amplitude and power, signal-to-noise ratio, and asymmetry in different latency intervals. Further, since EP morphologies change as a function of age and stimulus parameters, since various components have been implicated as aberrant in certain groups of dysfunctional children, and since component identification is a procedure posing serious difficulties for even the most skilled investigators, a general method for objective evaluation of overall EP morphology appeared to be essential.

EP Indices of Maturation

A number of reports indicate that features of EP morphology serve as indices of maturation (Dustman and Beck 1969; Ellingson 1967a, b; Rhodes, Dustman, and Beck 1969; Rose and Ellingson 1970; Schenkenberg and Dustman 1970). Other reports have related EP features such as amplitude or asymmetry between homologous derivations to intelligence, acquisition of language skills, or performance of tasks requiring different concepts (Buchsbaum and Fedio 1969, 1970; Giannitrapani 1967; Perry and Childers 1969; Richlin et al. 1971; Rhodes, Dustman, and Beck 1969; Schenkenberg and Dustman 1970; Shelburne 1972; Vella, Butler, and Glass 1972). The relevance of these observations to evaluation of learning disabled children, and some indication of EP features possibly useful for such purposes, is apparent in a number of reports.

EP Assessment of Sensory Acuity

Adequate sensory input is a prerequisite to the development of adaptive behavior. EP optometric and audiometric measures are increasingly being used to obtain objective measures of acuity in children and in patients in whom verbal cooperation is difficult to achieve. Numerous workers have demonstrated that it is possible to use EPs in order to estimate auditory thresholds and the focusing of retinal images with adequate precision for diagnostic purposes (Barnet and Goodwin 1965; Barnet and Lodge 1966, 1967; Cody and Bickford 1965; Copenhaver and Perry 1964; Davis 1965, 1968; Davis et al. 1976; Eason, White, and Bartlett 1970; Engel and Young 1969; Harter 1971; Harter and White 1968, 1970; Keidel and Spreng 1965, 1970; Mc-Candless 1967; Rapin and Graziani 1967; Rapin, Ruben, and Lyttle 1970). The relevant literature on evoked response audiometry has been well reviewed (Barnet 1972; Graziani and Weitzman 1972). Early detection of deafness in children is of special importance because of its implications for language acquisition and the urgency of early intervention (Gellis and Kagan 1970; O'Gorman 1962).

These methods of visual and auditory acuity assessment have been limited by the requirement that the presence of an EP be visually recognized by the examiner and that particular components be assessed. This process depends upon subjective judgments and inevitably generates ambiguous results. Recognizing this limitation, efforts have been made to devise objective statistical procedures for these purposes, with some success (John 1974; John, Ruchkin, and Vidal 1978). On the basis of the prior work, it seemed desirable and possible to develop standardized EP methods for assessment of visual and auditory acuity by statistical evaluation of certain features. Plausible features included the signal-to-noise ratio of EPs within specified latency intervals in particular derivations or the statistical significance of the difference between two EPs recorded from the same, selected derivation in response to auditory stimuli above and below normal hearing threshold or in response to check sizes above and below the visual resolution of the normal eye.

EP Assessment of Perception

It has been well demonstrated that the shape of the EP in primary sensory regions changes when stimuli of different geometric form but equal area are presented (Clynes, Kohn, and Gradijan 1967; Fields 1969; Herrington and Schneidau 1968; John, Herrington, and Sutton 1967; Pribram, Spinelli, and Kamback 1967). Stimuli of the same shape produce similar waveshapes independent of stimulus size (Clynes, Kohn, and Gradijan 1967; Hudspeth and Jones 1971; John 1974; John, Herrington, and Sutton 1967).

These observations indicate that differences between the contours of stimuli of different shapes, if they are perceived as different, will produce differences between the corresponding EPs, reflecting the innate brain mechanisms involved in processing contour information. Evaluation of differences between occipital EPs elicited by different shapes might reveal whether they produced different sensations. Evaluations of differences in parietal, posterior temporal, and central EPs might reveal whether information about these different sensations produced different effects in regions involved in generating perceptions about the sensations (Grinberg and John 1974; John 1976; John 1977; Johnston and Chesney 1974). Further, the recognition that large and small forms of the same shape share an invariant property and are identified by the same word is an acquired ability, corresponding to shape invariance. Such equivalence is built upon the accumulation of experience that distant objects bear visual similarities to the same objects nearby. EP measures of shape invariance might provide estimates of the development of this perceptual capability and its semantic correlate, reflected in various brain regions.

For these reasons, it seemed desirable to include stimuli of different shapes but equal area in our EP assessment of learning disabled children. Since geometric forms are perhaps more readily discriminated than letters of the alphabet, and since many children seem to have a special problem with accurate perception of certain letters such as *b* and *d,* it seemed that both geometric and alphabet forms should be used as stimuli. In addition, in order to assess shape invariance, it seemed worthwhile to study EPs elicited by the same geometric forms of different sizes.

EP Assessment of Cognitive Processes

Although maturational lag, inadequate sensory acuity, or perceptual difficulties may be the source of the learning disabilities of many children, it seems particularly important to seek evoked potential techniques which might directly reflect cognitive processes. Ideally, such EP techniques should provide an insight into how a child naturally gathers and uses information from his environment, without imposing an overt learning task. A number of EP phenomena reported in the literature seem well suited to probe such processes.

Control of Afferent Input

Habituation is a general property of many functional systems of the brain. Powerful centrifugal mechanisms exist that can exclude, from the higher levels of the brain, afferent input related to informationally trivial events. The anatomy and functional characteristics of this system have been studied extensively in a wide variety of nervous systems (John 1961). A distinction can be made between short-term or *phasic* and long-term or *tonic* aspects of habituation, which can be related to different anatomical structures, particularly the cortex, the reticular formation of the brain stem, and the diffuse projection nuclei of the thalamus (Dunlop et al. 1964; Fernandez-Guardiola et al. 1961; Key 1965; Marsh and Worden 1964; Sharpless and Jasper 1956). Hernandez-Peon, a pioneer in the study of habituation, argued that this phenomenon represents a rudimentary form of learning, requiring sufficient memory to recognize a present event as one that was inconsequential in the past (Hernandez-Peon, Scherrer, and Jouvet 1956).

Broad general limits have been established for the rate of habituation of sensory EPs in man (Endroczi et al. 1968; Fruhstorfer, Soveri, and Jarvilehto 1970). In a particularly interesting paper, Barnet and her colleagues demonstrated that children with certain brain disorders show little or no habituation, and can reliably be differentiated from normal children by the age of one year (Barnet and Lodge 1967). Other investigators have reported little or no habituation in hyperactive compared with normal children (Stevens, Sachdev, and Milstein 1968;

Tizard 1968). Such observations suggest that some learning disabled children may lack the ability to inhibit irrelevant afferent input and may possibly have defects in short-term memory, and that EP measures of habituation may provide a method to identify this defect.

Construction of Expectancy

It has long been known that while a subject awaits an anticipated event, a widespread negative potential gradually increases over many brain regions, the so-called contingent negative variation or CNV (Walter et al. 1964). When a stimulus is embedded in an unpredictable sequence, a late positive component at about 300 milliseconds latency (P300) is present in the EP; this component is markedly diminished or absent when the stimulus modality and time of occurrence can be predicted by the subject (Sutton et al. 1967, 1965). A great volume of experimental work has explored the CNV and the late positive components of the EP (LPC), and the possible relationship between these two different electrophysiological reflections of a prediction about the future based upon evaluation of the past (for review, see Donchin et al. 1975).

The brain seems to construct a representation of recent events that is used to generate expectations about future events. Late positive components reflect the matching of these predictions against ongoing events. The amplitude of LPCs seems to be greater when the probability of the expected event is low. Match-mismatch operations are involved in the response to novelty, the focusing of attention, the phenomenon of habituation, the classification of events and the organization of memory, as well as in interpreting symbols and establishing word meaning (Posner et al. 1973; Thatcher and John 1977).

The brain can apparently produce a facsimile of the usual response to an absent stimulus (Barlow, Morrell, and Morrell 1967a, b; Herrington and Schneidau 1967; John 1963, 1967a, b; John et al. 1967, 1973; John, Ruchkin, and Sachs 1967; Klinke,

Fruhstorfer, and Finkenzeller 1968; Ruchkin and John 1966; Sutton et al. 1967). Some workers refer to such endogeneously produced potentials as readout processes (John 1973, 1976; John et al. 1973) or as emitted potentials (Ruchkin and Sutton 1973; Weinberg, Walter, and Crow 1970). Further, other evidence indicates that the shape of the EP to semantic stimuli depends upon their context or meaning rather than their form (Brown, Marsh, and Smith 1973, 1976). Evidence also established that early short latency parts of the EP waveshape depend primarily upon the physical characteristics of the stimulus (exogenous), while late long latency parts of the waveshape depend primarily on the context in which the stimulus is perceived or the meaning assigned to it (endogenous). Several papers demonstrated that the contribution of exogenous and endogenous activity to the EP waveshape varies from head region to head region (Bartlett and John 1973; Grinberg and John 1974; John 1977; Johnston and Chesney 1974). Primary sensory cortex waveshapes are dominated by exogenous processes, while association cortex displays more contribution from endogenous processes.

These considerations suggested that it might be possible to evaluate the generation of expectancies and predictions in children by comparing EPs to predictable and unpredictable events. The contribution of exogenous and endogenous processes to EP waveshapes in such conditions, as well as in evaluation of size invariance discussed earlier, might be estimated in different regions by separately assessing *early,* short latency and *late,* long latency features of the EP waveshape. Differences between normal children and some subgroup of learning disabled children might reasonably be expected to appear from such measurements.

Structure of Figure-Ground Relations

A critical difficulty of many learning disabled children may consist of the inability to identify useful sources of information in the surroundings or to construct meaningful figure-ground relationships (Birch 1964). This deficiency would at best produce a lower signal-to-noise ratio for important information due to higher variability of the focus of attention or mixing of relevant and irrelevant inputs, and might at worst totally vitiate the potential utility of informationally relevant events because attention was misdirected to background noise. Some evidence shows that EP studies can cast light on the structure of figure-ground relations. In a classical paper, Hernandez-Peon et al. showed that the EP elicited by a click in the cochlear nucleus of a cat was dramatically inhibited while the cat watched a mouse in a beaker (Hernandez-Peon, Scherrer, and Jouvet 1956). This observation clearly illustrated that relevant afferent input in one sensory modality can inhibit irrelevant input in another modality. Other evidence demonstrated that relevant input (listening to verbal material) can suppress irrelevant input (clicks) even within the same sensory modality (Morrell and Morrell 1965). Abundant more recent evidence established that such enhancement or suppression of EPs in part or whole can be produced by a mental set, in which only part of a stimulus complex is important to the subject (for review, see John 1977a).

These findings provide support for the belief that properly devised conditions might yield EP measures reflecting the dynamic structuring of figure-ground relationships in different brain regions of a child. It seems reasonable to expect that some learning-disabled children differ significantly from normal children with respect to these processes.

EP Assessment of Conditioning

A vast literature demonstrates that numerous changes in the EEG and EP take place during learning (for reviews, see John and Schwartz 1978; Leiman and Cristian 1973; Thatcher and John 1977). Most of these studies involve the establishment of a new conditioned instrumental response and involve relatively lengthy procedures unsuitable for routine evaluation of children. However, a particularly intriguing subset of these studies is represented by sensory-sensory conditioning, sometimes referred to as cortical conditioning because it is manifested as cortical electrical activity (John 1967b; Morrell and Jasper 1956).

The essential feature of sensory-sensory conditioning is that if two sensory stimuli of different quality are presented simultaneously or with a short interval between them, after a number of such associations or pairings the presentation of one of these stimuli elicits the electrophysiological correlates of presentation of the other. The conditioned response, in other words, consists in that one stimulus comes to produce some of the effects of the other on brain electrical activity.

The fact that this type of conditioning requires no behavioral response or cooperation, needs no instructions, can be established in one session of about fifteen minutes, and can be objectively evaluated by EP measures makes it especially attractive for the direct assessment of learning in children. It seems reasonable to expect that an electrophysiological measure of associative learning, which is an essential process in categorizing experiences, would reveal abnormal features in many learning disabled children.

The Neurometric Battery

Having examined this EEG and EP literature potentially relevant to objective identification and diagnosis of brain dysfunction in learning disabled children, we concluded that many conditions and measures had been described that might be useful for these purposes. However, it was not at all clear which of these various assessment procedures might be most informative, which electrode placements would provide the clearest insights in the largest percentage of children, or which features of the EEG and EP would reveal clinically useful information about brain functions. The problem seemed too important and the uncertainties too large for hazardous reliance on our intuitions or prejudices (read "knowledge").

Rather than select a few procedures, placements, and measures on which to place our bets, we felt that current computer technology not only justified but compelled a more comprehensive approach. We constructed a set of test items that included examples of every type of assessment that seemed feasible to achieve by electrophysiological methods, and combined them into what we called the Neurometric Battery or NB (John et al. 1977a, b; John 1977).

It should be noted that the NB was designed to have broad general applicability regardless of age, intellectual level, or cooperativeness of the patient. This allows a single metric to be applicable across ages, as well as enabling testing of patients previously intractable to testing. In order to accomplish this, an approach using *passive "challenges"* of brain function was used. That is, the child was not required to respond to any item, to problem-solve or follow complex instructions. He or she was only required to observe the stimuli that were presented.

We designed and built an automatic Digital Electrophysiological Data Acquisition and Analysis System (DEDAAS), which contained software to administer the test items of the NB in a standardized way, using a computer-controlled stimulator. DEDAAS simultaneously gathered EEGs or EPs from the full nineteen channels of the International 10/20 Electrode System (Jasper 1958), recorded as monopolar data referenced to linked earlobes. On-line artifact rejection algorithms automatically rejected data contaminated by artifacts, and data acquisition continued until adequate samples of acceptable data had been obtained. These samples were stored in digital format, accompanied by digitally encoded protocols to permit subsequent automatic retrieval and analysis of the data. Upon retrieval, any desired monopolar or bipolar derivations could be reconstructed. Analysis software was written to extract a wide variety of features of potential clinical utility from these data and to permit evaluation of the distributions of such features in different populations, relative to some normative reference.* Finally, the NB was administered to a large sample of normal and learning disabled children, the resulting data subjected to conventional analyses as well as feature extraction, and the different procedures, placements, and features evaluated for their utility in detection and diagnosis of brain dysfunctions in learning disabled children. All NB items were administered to every child studied in early stages of our work, but only selected items to children studied in later stages. This monograph presents details of our methods and the comparisons of data obtained from groups of normal and learning disabled children using each item in the NB.

*Numerous instruments that incorporate the features of DEDAAS are now commercially available. One of these (Spectrum 32, Cadwell Laboratories, Kennewick, Washington) provides a *Neurometric Analyzer* licensed from New York University.

CHAPTER 3

Methods

Subjects

Normal subjects (*N* = 636) consisted of 398 males and 238 female children from five to sixteen years of age, most of whom were recruited as paid ($10.00) volunteers responding to newspaper notices and a few of whom were purely voluntary subjects reflecting community interest in the research project. A subject was accepted for entry in the normal group (N) if he or she were and had always been at grade level in all academic subjects, had no history of pre- or perinatal problems, head injury or neurological diseases, were not taking any prescription medications, and scored in the normal range on intelligence (above 85 on Wechsler Intelligence Scales for Children [WISC] and/or above 90 on Peabody Picture Vocabulary Test [PPVT]) and had standard scores of 90 or above on achievement (Wide Range Achievement Test [WRAT]) tests. A normal subgroup meeting all of the above requirements but showing underachievement on WRAT scores was also identified for study (normal underachievers).

Learning Disabled subjects (*N* = 1,113) consisted of 905 males and 208 female children from five to twenty-one years of age, most of whom were recruited from schools in and around New York City. Some of these children had *specific* learning disabilities (SLD), and others had *generalized* learning disabilities (LD). These usually came from a special school for learning disabled children (James E. Allen Learning Center, Dix Hills, New York). A subject was considered acceptable for the SLD group if he or she were at least two years below grade level on at least one academic subject, had no sensory handicap or untreated neurological disease, had an intelligence test score of 85 or above, and showed severe underachievement in at least one specific area on achievement tests (standard scores below 85 on the WRAT). There was also identified for study an SLD subgroup meeting all these requirements but without underachievement on WRAT scores (SLD overachievers).

A subject was considered acceptable for the LD group if he or she were at least two years below grade level on several academic subjects, had no sensory handicap or untreated neurological disease, had an intelligence test score between 60 and 84, and showed generalized underachievement on achievement tests (standard scores below 85 on the WRAT). Table 1 shows mean psychometric scores for these different groups. (For all tables see appendix 2.)

No children were accepted into the study if they were presently taking any prescription medication. Histories were assessed by detailed parental questionnaires. Children in normal groups had to supply report cards from the last two academic years as further certification of grade level achievement. All psychometric tests were administered by Brain Research Laboratory staff who were trained to appropriate levels of inter-rater reliability by a professional neuropsychologist on our staff. Letters explaining our purpose were distributed to all parents.

Recording Procedures

Upon arrival at the laboratory the children were shown around the room and test chamber. They were shown (and given to hold) an electrode, electrode cream, etc. They were then placed in front of a mirror for electrode placement so they could watch the procedure.

Nineteen electrodes were placed on each child, according to the International 10/20 System. Linked earlobes were used as the reference. Two electrodes, located above and right of the orbit, were used to record the electrooculogram (EOG). Silver-silver chloride disk electrodes were affixed to the scalp using electrode paste and covered with small gauze pads held in place by hair clips. Electrode impedances were tested before beginning the examination and were considered unacceptable if over 5,000 ohms. Electrode impedance was thereafter monitored by the computer to ensure that impedances did not increase.

Due to the wide range of ages and intellectual levels of these children, and since the Neurometric Battery was specifically constructed to require minimal cooperation, rather than presenting a fixed set of instructions to the children, our staff made certain points to the child (using their experience and judgment to decide how to make those points). The essential points to be covered for each child were:

1. nature and purpose of NB in general terms;
2. importance of trying to move as little as possible, and to refrain as much as possible from blinking or clenching teeth;
3. importance of looking at the fixation point on the screen before them when asked to do so;
4. reassurance that there would be frequent rest periods during which the child would be allowed to move and blink freely.

During the recording sessions, a member of the laboratory or a parent sat next to the child. This was to relax and reassure the child and remind him or her to keep his or her eyes open or closed as instructed. In addition, the observer filled out a questionnaire rating the child's behavior during the test. The children were all informed that the recording session could be interrupted or terminated at any time if they did not wish to continue. Since the full NB takes almost two hours to administer, requests to interrupt became more probable as the recording session went on. Most normal children, however, resumed the recording willingly after a short period of rest and refreshment, while many learning disabled children decided to terminate the session. As a result, our sample size on items occurring early in the NB accumulated more rapidly than for later items. After a sufficient body of data had been gathered on early items, the item sequence was changed so that items for which a paucity of data had been gathered were presented earlier in the sequence. After an initial period in which all NB items were evaluated, only certain selected NB items were studied in a larger group of children.

Stimulus Conditions: The Neurometric Battery

The full Neurometric Battery contained 115 test items. Some of these items consisted of the EEG or EP recorded under specific conditions, and are referred to as *conditions*. Other items consisted of comparisons between EEG or EPs recorded from the same site under two different conditions, where the change in the electrophysiological measurement associated with the difference between the conditions was the feature of interest. Such items are referred to as *challenges*. The conditions and challenges of the NB were grouped into ten sets, each intended to probe a different aspect of brain function (John 1977; John et al. 1977b). These sets, the conditions and challenges comprising them, and the intent of each item are given in full in appendix 1.

Set I provides estimates of structural integrity and functional maturation by quantitative analysis of EEG features. These studies yielded equations that describe the normal development of a large number of features of brain electrical activity across the age range from six to sixteen, subsequently extended from six to ninety years. Cognitively, neurologically, and psychiatrically normal individuals show few deviations from predicted values of these features, while dysfunctional patients display numerous significant deviations. The sensitivity and specificity of these developmental equations has already been confirmed in seven different countries, indicating that they describe features of brain electrical activity which are culture fair and independent of ethnic background, yet sensitive to even subtle disturbances (chap. 6).

Set II studies the effectiveness of photic driving at frequencies in the center of four different EEG frequency bands. This provides an index of the ease of reorganizing the transactions between different neuroanatomical systems reflected by the EEG spectrum. Set III studies the speed of habituation of the EEG to assess how quickly a subject adjusts to a meaningless perturbation. Set IV compares EP responses to predictable versus unpredictable stimulus sequences, to assess the ability of the subject to detect and predict order in temporal relations among different sensory stimuli. Set V uses the rate of diminution of EP responses to repeated stereotypic stimulus sequences to measure the speed and amount of habituation that reflects the ability to ignore irrelevant events, the effectiveness with which novel events can achieve dishabituation that reflects adequate monitoring of the environment, and the speed of rehabituation that reflects retention of the prior experience and recognition of its return.

Using EP methods, Set VI estimates sensory acuity and effects of contrast, Set VII assesses brain mechanisms related to shape perception and size invariance, and Set VIII evaluates brain mechanisms related to letter perception. In conjunction with the information from Sets VI and VII, this permits reading disabilities such as letter reversal to be decomposed into acuity deficits, perceptual deficits, and deficits in verbal labeling of visual symbols.

Set IX assesses the subject's ability to structure figure-ground relations in a way that appropriately segregates meaningful information from noise. Set X evaluates the ability of the subject to establish learned associations between events in different sensory modalities.

Digital Electrophysiological Data Acquisition and Analysis System (DEDAAS)

Amplifiers
All data were recorded by amplifiers we constructed, which had a fixed gain of 10,000, with 106 dB common mode rejection, an

input impedance of 10 megohms, a noise level with shorted inputs of 2 μV peak to peak, and a frequency response which had 3 dB points at 0.5 and 30 Hz, using filters with an attentuation of 42 dB per octave. Our initial amplifiers had a photically coupled first stage, to permit them to be used safely in premature infant intensive care units. A circuit for this version has been published (John 1977). In later versions for additional terminals (which were not to be used in ICUs), the front end was redesigned to eliminate the photic coupling.

Analog-to-Digital Conversion
The analog-to-digital converter yielded 10 significant bits for an input range of ± 2.5 V. This was shifted down to 8 significant bits, and rounded, in which form the data was stored on digital tape. Thus, the resolution of the stored data corresponded to about 2 μV at the electrode, or about the same as the amplifier noise.

Computer Control
DEDAAS was initially implemented with the data acquisition functions mediated by a PDP 11/10 minicomputer terminal with 8 K words of core, a real-time clock, an analog-to-digital converter, a 16-bit general purpose I/O interface to control the stimulators, a video display, and a magnetic tape unit for data storage. The system could run two subjects independently at the same time, to a maximum of 32 channels altogether. This limitation was imposed by the microprocessor speed. When additional terminals were needed, the software was revised to be mediated by an LSI 11/03 microprocessor system that included an LSI 11/03 microprocessor, 16 KB of memory, a 12-bit analog-to-digital converter, a real-time clock, a video display, an I/O interface for stimulus control, and a dual disk drive for floppy disks. Data was collected on floppy disks in soft sector format. The real-time clock frequency was 100 Hz. A special purpose, real-time operating system was used in order to allow acquisition and preprocessing with the maximum

speed. This operating system supported an on-line interpreter. This interpreter allowed experiment reprogramming, stimulus sequence changes, data collection, and changes in the rate of data displays.

Automatic On-Line Artifact Rejection

At the beginning of each recording session, the DEDAAS operator observed the EEG on an oscilloscope, looking for a period with relatively large amplitude alpha activity in the posterior leads, with minimal eye movement while the subject was resting quietly with eyes closed. The importance of waiting until posterior alpha activity appears must be emphasized. A tense subject will display a desynchronized EEG with little alpha. The selection of such data as the criterion sample will result in rejection of later samples after relaxation as spurious artifacts because of increased alpha. When such a period occurred, the operator depressed a key on the computer terminal and the next five seconds of EEG were sampled. Mean square amplitudes and standard deviations were computed across that EEG segment for each of the 19 channels and the EOG channel. Individual amplitude limits were then set for each channel, using the mean squared amplitude plus five standard deviations in each direction.

If the EEG in any channel subsequently exceeded the *artifact threshold,* data from all channels were rejected until one second after the EEG returned below the threshold. During the artifact threshold setting procedure, the operator asked the subject to blink, move his or her eyes horizontally and vertically while the EOG was examined to be sure data would be artifacted at the level selected. (A maximum period of fifteen minutes was allowed to optimize artifact rejection criteria.) All acceptable data were recorded on a floppy disk.

In subjects from whom the complete EP battery was collected, a somewhat different artifact rejection method was used. In this method, data acquisition was suspended if the absolute value of the voltage in any of the derivations or in the

EOG channel exceeded a specified value, and for a further half second after the cessation of such a condition. The threshold voltages were set by the operator at the beginning of the session. Separate thresholds were entered for the frontal leads $(F_1F_2F_7F_8)$, for the remaining leads, and for the EOG channel. Each of the above was specified twice, first for a strict criterion, and then for a looser criterion, with higher values. The subject was normally run at the strict criterion; but if data acquisition in any condition was slowed severely by artifact rejection (i.e., if ten minutes real time elapsed), a switch on the console caused the criterion to be changed to a looser one. All acceptable data were recorded on magnetic media. It should be noted that the two methods of artifact rejection described above produced equivalent results. Test-retest data of learning disabled children is also relevant to this comparison of on-line artifact rejection methods, in that children tested with one method and retested with another showed invariant clinical profiles (see chap. 4, "Test-Retest" sec.).

On-line Computation of EPs and Variances
As each stimulus was presented by the stimulator, DEDAAS sampled the electrical signal in each of the 19 channels, at 10-millisecond intervals. Each sample X_i was squared, and the sums of X_i and X_i^2 *were computed for an epoch of 100 intervals, i.e., one second. These sums were accumulated for each EP condition, and the average and variance computed at each latency point. The average EOG was also computed for each condition. Each condition thus generated 1,900 words defining the EPs and 1,900 words defining the variances, which were stored, together with information identifying the recording channels and that stimulus condition, on the floppy disk. The average EOG from each condition was also stored.*

Digital Storage
In the original DEDAAS, neurometric records were stored on a 1,600 BPI Wang digital tape drive, model Wangco 9TKPE-NEZI. This unit proved unacceptably troublesome and prone to

malfunction. As a result, subsequent terminals were built using a Charles River Data System dual floppy disk drive model A 10PE, which proved far more reliable and troublefree. When the reduced version of the NB was used, one subject's data occupied two floppy disks.

Visual Editing of EEG Record

After the NB was recorded, the disks were brought to the computer center of the Brain Research Laboratories for analysis, which was carried out on either a PDP 11/45 or 11/34 minicomputer system. The first step in analysis was to read the floppy disk into the computer, transcribing it onto digital magnetic tapes that could hold large numbers of such NB records. The raw data record was then written out on a Versatec matrix printer, yielding a 19-channel graphic reproduction of the total EEG record, and the EPs and variances from all NB conditions. This record included a sequential elapsed time base, marked every 200 milliseconds. The EEG record was then examined by experienced EEG technicians who noted the time intervals during which any visible artifacts contaminated the record, having eluded the computer's artifact-rejection algorithm. An *edit file* was then constructed, indicating all contaminated EEG segments, which were deleted from the digital EEG record prior to further analysis. The EPs and variances were also examined to identify any averages with spurious waveshapes, unusually high variances, or significant average EOGs, indicating the presence of possible artifacts in those records. Such spurious data were also removed from the record. See figure 1 for a flow chart of the DEDAAS.

Data Analysis System

Subsequent to editing, data analysis was performed on our PDP 11/45 minicomputer system. Our software was written to be used with the UNIX operating system developed by Bell Telephone Laboratories. The system configuration required to uti-

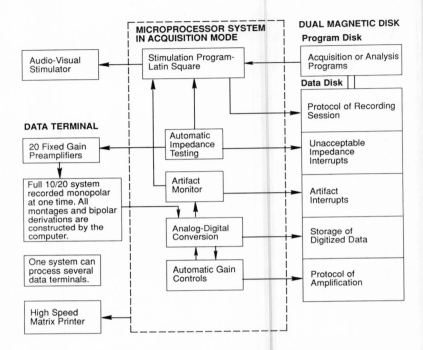

Fig. 1.   Digital Electrophysiological Data Acquisition and
Analysis System

lize these programs was as follows: PDP 11/45 with memory management and 96 K words of core, a magnetic tape unit, a large disk for temporary storage (at least 80 KB capacity), and a Versatec matrix printer plotter for graphics output (10 inches wide, with resolution of 200 dots per inch). (It is ironic that the capabilities of this system, which represented the state of the art when we built it, were an order of magnitude less than that which is now available in most personal computers for a fraction of the cost.)

The software used for data acquisition in DEDAAS and for data analysis with the algorithms described below can be obtained for research purposes by special arrangements with New

York University, which has licensed these methods for commercial use to Cadwell Laboratories, Kennewick, Washington, which now markets a *Neurometric Analyzer*.

EEG Analysis

Wide-band Digital Filtering

The numerical calculation of frequency domain measures was performed via the use of recursive digital filters, rather than by the more conventional use of the Fast Fourier Transform. This decision was made due to the computational advantages offered by recursive digital filtering technique in cases where the data may be modeled in terms of a small number of narrow-band generators. The digital filters used were Butterworth 4-pole bandpass and 2-pole low-pass recursive filters with 36 dB/octave roll-off. Complex demodulation, and decimation in frequency were used to reduce the computation requirements. The EEG pass-bands used were 1.5–3.5 Hz (delta), 3.5–7.5 Hz (theta), 7.5–12.5 Hz (alpha), and 12.5–25.0 Hz (beta).

Conversion of Absolute to Relative Power

Comparisons of test-retest reliability (within session) were made for a group of children in which we began and ended an hour-long evoked potential recording session by gathering a 60-second sample each of computer artifacted, eyes-open and eyes-closed EEG. Using absolute power measures in each frequency band, we found that replicability was relatively poor. Therefore, we transformed these measures to relative (percent) power by dividing the absolute power in each frequency band by the total power in all four bands, for each derivation. In contrast with the moderate replicability of our absolute power data, these relative power measures revealed excellent replicability, confirmed by others (Van Dis et al. 1977). Further, healthy children in a restricted age range showed a narrow range of relative power values, while learning disabled children of the same age often showed values far outside this range. Examining the distribution of relative power values in large samples of normal, healthy children, in order to develop valid statistical criteria for evaluating individual values, we found a logarithmic transform [log $X/(100 - X)$] achieved approximately Gaussian distributions for all relative power measures, justifying use of conventional parametric statistics. The adequacy of this transform has since been confirmed by Gasser, Bacher, and Mocks (1982), Fein et al. (1983), and Oken and Chiappa (1988).

Normative Developmental Polynomial Functions

Using sharply tuned analog bandpass filters and resting EEG (eyes closed) records tape recorded from a sample of 561 healthy male and female Swedish children, Matousek and Petersen (1973) computed the means and standard deviations of the amplitude of the EEG in the delta, theta, alpha, and beta bands in bilateral frontotemporal, central, temporal and parieto-occipital derivations (left and right hemisphere derivations were pooled) for age groups from one to twenty-one years old in yearly increments, and published normative tables.

The striking orderly nature of the normative tables, and our findings that relative power measures were replicable and sensitive, encouraged us to construct equations to describe maturational changes in the relative power of the EEG, to test their accuracy in different groups of children and to evaluate their sensitivity to brain disease or dysfunction. Our first step was to convert the mean values and standard deviations, published by Matousek and Petersen (1973), to relative power (John 1977; Van Dis et al. 1977), and then to transform these data by $Y = \log X/(100 - X)$. We then took advantage of the full body of data to minimize irregularities reflecting age truncation, small sample sizes, and sampling errors at each age, and computed a polynomial regression equation for each EEG parameter in each derivation. The transformed data were fitted with sixth-order orthogonal (Chebyshev) polynomials (Korn and Korn 1968). Analysis of F tests revealed that there were many significant contributions by terms up to the fourth order, but insignificant contributions ($<$ 1 percent) to the variance above that. The equations were reduced to standard polynomials of the form:

$$Y = C_0 + C_1 t + C_2 t^2 + C_3 t^3 + C_4 t^4, \text{ where } t = \text{age (in years)} - 1.0.$$

Thus, we obtained sixteen equations for delta, theta, alpha, and beta in frontotemporal, temporal, central, and parieto-occipital derivations, each with five coefficients.

Since the frequency response of our amplifiers, the objective nature of our computer artifact rejection, and the sharpness of our digital filters represented important possible sources of difference from the work of Matousek and Petersen (1973), we tried to develop an empirical correction to relate the two data sets. Using demographically diverse groups of 48 normal children from New York City, we computed the mean values for each of the sixteen EEG parameters, regressing all data to the group mean age of 10.6 years. Small differences were found between the resulting means and those predicted for that age by the sixteen equations. Each of these differences was used to provide a calibration term C_0 for the corresponding equation. C_0 represents the correction necessary to compensate for constant shifts arising from small differences in equipment specifications or analytical methods, *and must be ascertained by a corresponding calibration procedure for any system in which these equations are to be used.*

Examining the log-transformed normative data further, we noted that the differing values of the standard deviations were strikingly close to a constant, differing with each measure but independent of age. The physical, ethnic, and cultural heterogeneity of the children we intended to study was far greater than the carefully screened and relatively homogenous Swedish group from which the normative tables were derived. Further, the published data (Matousek and Petersen 1973) did not allow the computation of standard deviations for relative power. Thus, we were forced to rely on our data for variance information. In our data, the variability of individual values around the predicted values yielded a standard deviation about 1.5 times larger for each EEG parameter than that reported for the Swedish children. Based on our observations that the standard deviation was approximately constant across age for each EEG parameter in the Swedish data after log transform, initially, we assumed that the standard deviations thus obtained for our 10.6-year age group could be validly extended across the whole age range. Using all later data, the coefficients for each of the thirty-two polynomials that predicted the log-transformed relative power in each frequency band for every derivation (left and right side derivations were described separately), and the corresponding actual standard deviations, were subsequently published (John et al. 1980).

Coherence and Power Asymmetry Measures

The coherence and asymmetry measures were computed as follows: First, the parameters r and q were computed as the normalized cross-spectra between bilateral pairs at each frequency. r was the real component; q was the quadrature component. Both should be between -1 and $+1$. The coherence, COH, was then defined as:

$$COH = \sqrt{r^2 + q^2}$$

The time difference, $TDEL$, was then computed (in milliseconds) as:

$$TDEL = \frac{159.1549 \; TAN - 1 \; (q/r)}{SC}$$

where SC equaled the center frequency of the particular band.

Asymmetry, $ASYM$, between the right and left sides was computed as:

$$ASYM = 200 \, (PL - PR)/(PL + PR)$$

where PL = spectral power on the left side and PR = spectral power on the right side.

To compute the normative data and Z scores for these parameters, the data were first transformed to approximately Gaussian measures and then the means and standard deviations were computed, with the standard Z-score computation performed on these transformed measures (for details see John et al. 1983, 1987).

Z-transform of EEG Features

$$Z_i = [Y_i - (\overline{Y}_i - C)]/\sigma_i$$

represents the Z transform, which gives the probability of obtaining the observed value for a particular EEG parameter Y_i in that anatomical derivation i in a normal healthy child of age t by chance, where Y_i = the log transform of the individual's EEG relative power measures; $\overline{Y}_i$ = the expected value for age t from the regression equations derived from our log-transformed norms; C = calibration term that represents the correction necessary to compensate for constant shifts arising from small differences in equipment specification and analytical methods between our laboratory and Matousek and Petersen's laboratory; and σ_i = the log-transformed standard deviation of our normative sample for that parameter.

Maturational Lag as Differentiated from Developmental Deviation
The vector sum of Z scores of the four frequency bands was computed for each region. Distributions of these sums have been constructed on a large population; and an algorithm has been written that accesses, for any statistically significant vector sum, whether there is an age for which it is nonsignificant. If so, it defines this as the *maturational lag* in years. If there is no age at which this vector sum is nonsignificant, the profile is considered *developmentally deviant*. Details of these methods and findings have been published elsewhere (John et al. 1983).

EP Analysis

Average and Variance

Averaged evoked potentials (AEP) and the corresponding variance as a function of latency were obtained by averaging over 50 stimulus presentations, for epochs of 750 to 1,000 milliseconds. The interstimulus interval was 1 second for regular stimuli, and it ranged from 0.8 second to 1.4 seconds for random interval stimuli, in all test conditions.

At the time of acquisition, possible bias in the zero voltage level of the observed potentials was not controlled. To remove such effects, the AEPs for each subject and derivation were averaged over the full latency epoch and over all experiments, and those averages, taken as the dc bias for the derivation, were subtracted before quantitative measures were calculated.

Evoked Potential Feature Analysis

The following measures were calculated for the evoked potentials. (The measures utilized were selected from a larger set that was explored.) Each measure was calculated over four subepochs: 50–120 ms, 120–300 ms, 300–500 ms, 0–500 ms. The measures were log transformed to yield approximately Gaussian distributions. Logarithms were taken to base e.

1. Power was measured by log mean power. The power was defined as the square of the amplitude.
2. Signal-to-noise ratio was measured by log maximum signal-to-noise ratio. The signal-to-noise ratio was defined as the power divided by the variance.
3. Waveshape symmetry was measured by log $(1 - r)/(1 + r)$ where r was the correlation coefficient between homologous left and right derivation pairs.
4. Wave power symmetry was measured by log mean difference power. The difference power was defined as the square of the amplitude difference between a left-right derivation pair.

5. Signal-to-noise symmetry was measured by log maximum difference signal-to-noise ratio. The difference in signal-to-noise ratio was defined as the difference power divided by the smaller variance of the two derivations involved. This was found to yield more stable data than using the mean of the two variances in the denominator.

Mahalanobis Distance

Another measure, called the Mahalanobis distance, was used to provide a general indication of the divergence of the shape of a test subject AEP from the normal control population, rather than testing specific predefined features such as the previously mentioned measures.

We assume that the AEPs of the normal population followed a multivariate normal distribution. The probability density for an observation Y_i (where the subscript represents the latency value) is:

$$P(Y_i) = A \exp - \sum_j \sum_k (Y_j - \overline{X}_j) \, C_{jk}^{-1} (Y_k - \overline{X}_k).$$

Here $\overline{X}_j$ is the true mean for a normal population,

$$\overline{X}_j = E(X_j),$$

and C^{-1} is the inverse of the covariance matrix

$$\begin{aligned} C_{jk} &= E\left[(X_j - \overline{X}_j)(X_k - \overline{X}_k)\right] \\ &= E(X_j X_k) - E(X_j)E(X_k). \end{aligned}$$

The logarithm of the exponent of the above distribution function $P(Y_i)$ should be approximately Gaussian in distribution, and may be treated as a measure similar to the others.

However, we did not have the true mean and covariance of the normal population, since our information came from a limited sample. The best estimates we could make were:

$$\overline{X}_i = \frac{1}{N} \sum_i X_i$$

$$C_{ij} = \frac{1}{N-1} \sum (X_i - \overline{X}_i)(X_j - \overline{X}_j)$$

where the sums are over the normal control population, of size N.

If we used these estimates, however, the procedure did not work very well for the normal control sample size that was available (about 120). The problem was that degrees of freedom of low variance in the covariance matrix became dominant when we computed the inverse, and sampling fluctuations in these degrees of freedom blurred the result. The procedure was improved by taking a modified inverse based on principle factor analyses.

By means of factor analysis, the covariance matrix could be expressed as the sum:

$$C_{ij} = \sum_m \lambda_m f^m_i f^m_j$$

where f^m_i was the mth principal factor and λ_m was the associated variance. The inverse could be written as

$$C^{-1}_{ij} \sum_m \lambda_m^{-1} f^m_i f^m_j.$$

Instead of this, we used the modified inverse

$$C^{-1}_{ij} \text{ (modified)} = \sum_{m=1}^{N_c} \lambda_m^{-1} f^m_i f^m_j + \sum_{m=N_c+1}^{N} \lambda_{nc}^{-1} f^m_i f^m_j,$$

where N_c was a cutoff value that was determined empirically. The effect of this was to limit the size of the λ^{-1} term in the sum.

After experimentation with the free parameters, we settled on a subepoch of 100 to 260 milliseconds for this measure, with a cutoff at 12. No attempt was made to compensate for subject age, since a linear regression method would not work in this situation.

The sensitivity and specificity of these Mahalanobis distance measures are evaluated relative to the more conventional EP feature decriptors (chap. 8).

Subject Population

All subjects whose data will be discussed herein were between six and sixteen years old, inclusive. For each NB condition, the subject population was divided into four groups.

1. Normal control group
2. Normal test group
3. LD group
4. SLD group

Note: Different children comprised these four groups for different NB conditions. The size of these groups also varied, as discussed in chapter 4.

Z Transform

The data from the normal control group was used to derive the population statistics for normal subjects. First, each measure was corrected for subject age by linear regression. The mean and standard deviation were then calculated for each of the age-regressed measures, over the normal control population.

The measures for all subjects in the other three groups were then regressed for age, using the coefficients derived from Group 1. These age corrected measures were then transformed into Z scores by subtracting the corresponding Group 1 mean and dividing by the Group 1 standard deviation.

Hit Matrix Score

The Z-transformed measures for selected subepochs for each EP condition were printed out in matrix form for each subject. The columns of the matrix corresponded to the derivations. Each cell is a particular *stimulus-measure-subepoch* combination. A threshold Z value and a choice of sign were specified. Only those matrix elements of the correct sign, with absolute value greater than the threshold, were printed: the rest were suppressed. Marginal totals of the number of superthreshold values in each row and column and overall were also printed. Finally, a summary matrix for each group of subjects gave the total number of superthreshold Z scores for all subjects in the group as well as marginal totals.

CHAPTER 4

EEG Measures in
Normal Children

Test Feasibility

The full NB (described in app. 1) takes about two to two and one-half hours to administer, depending upon the amount of time out due to computer artifact rejection because of movement. Since the full test proved to be fatiguing, it was administered in its entirety to 20 normal children to permit analysis of the factor structure of the battery as a whole. Another 150 normal and learning disabled children were tested on different subsets or combinations of NB items. The goal of these studies was to gather sufficient data to evaluate the utility and practicality of each NB condition and challenge, without imposing such severe demands for cooperation and patience that our results from items administered early would be more valid than those from items administered later in the session. After about an hour and fifteen minutes, learning disabled children were definitely more likely to request termination of the session than normal children. Once this was realized, each session was begun with a *core battery* of test items that took from thirty minutes to an hour to administer, depending on the cooperation and self-control of the subject. After the core data were recorded, the remaining time was spent proceeding in the sequence defined in the battery (see app. 1). As soon as the subject became restless and the incidence of computer artifact interrupts increased, the session was terminated. Thus, the length of the recording session varied from child to child, but lasted as long as the subject was able to provide valid data.

Obviously, the effect of this procedure was to increase the total size of the sample of available data more rapidly for early than for late items in the sequence. As the sample size for each early test item became sufficient for our purposes, that item was omitted from subsequent recording sessions. Thus, test items that were early in the sequence were administered to most of the initial children studied and then gradually replaced by test items that were later in the sequence, which were administered to a higher proportion of the children studied later. The effect of this procedure was to distribute the time at which most test items were administered from late to early within the set of sessions within which the item was included. We preferred this deliberate linking of item selection to sample size to a randomization procedure that might have better balanced effects of recency, order, and fatigue but might well have failed to produce sufficient data to evaluate every NB item within the limits of time and funds available for this work to be done.

It is important to stress that, as a result of this procedure, *the actual individuals who comprise the sample of normal and of learning disabled children are not the same from item to item.* The stability of our results, especially with regard to the Grand Average EP waveshapes, latencies, and leads at which certain effects were observed, becomes the more impressive if this is borne in mind. The actual sample size studied with each item can always be found in the tabular data. Our comprehensive evaluation of the NB comes from this relatively small subset of the much larger population from whom neurometric data have been collected.

Approximately 2,000 additional children have been studied with the core battery consisting of one minute of artifact-free, eyes-closed EEG, and computation of average EPs and variances to seven test items: checkerboards of 65, 27, and 7 lines per inch; the letters *b* and *d;* and regular as well as random 45 dB clicks. This core battery takes from thirty minutes to one hour to administer, depending on the incidence of computer artifact interrupts. It proved possible to gather the full set of core data on more than 98 percent of this group of children, comprised of about 500 normal and 1,500 learning disabled or neurologically ill children. The purpose of gathering these data was to develop a large data base across the age range six to sixteen years for the very fundamental probes contained in the core battery, so that accurate values for age-regressed EP features could be computed. When it seemed desirable to have access to data from more than the initial group of children studied, either to fill out sample sizes or to replicate promising findings, data from 242 children randomly selected from this large population were included in computing some of the results reported here. Much of the core data from the larger group, however, is still being analyzed. Further results will be presented in subsequent articles.

Finally, about 500 additional children have been tested using an expansion of the Neurometric Core Battery, or NB II. NB II was constructed by selecting those test items found to be most powerful for separation of normal and learning disabled children in the studies reported here, as well as being well tolerated by the children. The purpose of these examinations was to gather a set of data representing what we believe to be the optimum combination of electrophysiological measures to discriminate between normal and learning disabled children, to attempt to construct an accurate discriminant function for that purpose, and to replicate that successful discrimination (if achieved) in a carefully controlled, blinded study. Acquisition of those data has just concluded. The results of analyses of those data will be reported in subsequent articles. NB II consists of nineteen test items: one minute each of artifact-free, eyes-open and eyes-closed EEG, and computation of AEPs and variances to fifty stimuli delivered at a rate of 1 per second to the following stimuli: checkerboards of 65, 27, and 7 lines per inch; large square and diamond; the letters *b, d,* and *q;* flash delivered while looking at defocused video; flash delivered while looking at focused video; flash delivered while listening to a recording of rock music; 45 dB clicks; 45 dB clicks delivered at random intervals with an average rate of 1 per second; 45 dB clicks delivered while looking at defocused video; 45 dB clicks delivered while looking at focused video; 45 dB clicks delivered while listening to a recording of rock music; and a tactile stimulus (tap) delivered to the right ankle at random intervals with an average rate of 1 per second. NB II takes from about one hour to one and one-half hours to administer. It has been possible to gather full data on this set of measures on more than 95 percent of this group of children, consisting of one-half normal and one-half learning disabled subjects.

If the testing technicians are not abrupt and take pains to make friends, to explain the procedure, and to reassure the child, and if a front and rear mirror are provided to permit the child to watch the process of electrode placement, two technicians can prepare a child for recording in approximately thirty minutes. Although we have examined many extremely disturbed or hyperactive children, in only ten cases have we been unable to obtain at least the minimum useful measurement represented by a one-minute sample of computer artifact-free, eyes-closed EEG.

This monograph focuses upon the results obtained from 96 children subjected to different combinations of NB items in our initial studies and from 242 children subjected to the NB II. Findings from collaborative studies in several countries, in which neurometric analysis of the EEG was performed in large samples of normal and dysfunctional children, will also be summarized.

Validity of Automatic Artifact Rejection

The validity of data gathered by the computer program for automatic rejection of data contaminated by artifacts arising from eye movements, head movements, or other sources was evaluated. Two questions arise: first, does the artifact algorithm remove any segments of uncontaminated EEG that should have been retained as a legitimate part of the record? and second, if the record emerging from the automatic artifacting process is further subjected to visual editing in which contaminated portions of the EEG are additionally removed, does this systematically alter the individual profile of percent relative power? The first question is answerable in a straightforward manner. Several experts (experienced clinical neurophysiologists and EEG technicians) were asked to evaluate whether any segments on a set of EEG records previously marked for the presence of artifact using the computer algorithm but not deleted from the record would have been retained by the expert. Without exception, every "contaminated" detected segment selected by the computer algorithm would have been deleted by the human evaluation. However, there were sections of record acceptable to the computer that most of the experts would have removed. This leads to the second question: does visual "over-reading" of the machine-artifacted records introduce systematic bias? Since average response computation inherently defeats artifacts, randomizing them out and yielding a picture of the response that is most characteristic during the averaging period, we considered measures such as the frequency distribution in the resting, eyes-closed EEG likely to be more susceptible to distortion by artifacts. Accordingly, we randomly selected records of eyes-closed EEG from twenty children. To ensure that data from less cooperative learning disabled or hyperactive children were not less valid than measures obtained from more cooperative normal children, ten samples were taken from recordings of normal children and ten from LD children.

Spectral analyses were carried out on each of these recordings, using the full sample of data accepted as valid by the computer data acquisition system. These analyses provided measures of relative power in the delta, theta, alpha, and beta bands, and coherence and power asymmetry in each of these bands between eight bilaterally symmetrical (homologous) electrode derivations (F_7T_3/F_8T_4, T_3T_5/T_4T_6, C_3C_z/C_4C_z, P_3O_1/P_4O_2). Each recording is plotted as a paper record and subjected to visual editing by an experienced EEG technician. All EEG segments that might be considered as contaminated by artifacts not due to the electrical activity of the brain were removed. The remaining intervals of artifact-free EEG longer than 600 milliseconds (estimated response time of our digital filter algorithm) were again subjected to analyses, yielding the same set of measures on the visually edited, artifact-free EEG sample. Table 2 presents the value of the correlation coefficient between the two sets of data for 32 spectral estimators, separately for the normal and LD subgroups. Table 3 presents the correlations of the thirty-two measures of coherence and power asymmetry between the unedited and edited sample. Almost no significant differences were found between the computer edited data, and the human edited data, either with respect to the actual measures or the Z transforms of these measures relative to the means and standard deviations of our normative data base, as defined below.

Both for the normal and the LD groups, slightly less than 30 percent of the computer-artifacted record was deemed artifact contaminated upon visual examination. However, inspection of tables 2 (cols. A and B) and 3 shows that meticulous visual editing of all the contaminated segments by an experienced EEG technician had little effect on most of the quantitative measures yielded by our analytic procedures. This indicates that most artifacts with consistent features within the frequency range of our analysis had been excluded by the computer algorithms. Those that were found by the subsequent visual editing were not systematic, and had a random effect on the neurometric EEG measures. Further, most of the artifacts that had eluded the computer algorithm were either horizontal eye movements or muscle potentials (electromyograms, or EMG). Horizontal eye movements produce artifacts primarily in the 0.5 to 1.0 Hz domain, and EMG artifacts lie primarily in the 25 to 50 Hz domain. Since our analyses were restricted to the frequency range between 1.5 and 25.0 Hz, these artifacts had little effect. In spite of these findings, all of our EEG recordings are still routinely plotted graphically and visually edited before quantitative analyses are performed.

For normal subjects (col. A), the correlation between spectral estimators from unedited and edited EEG samples ranged from 0.961 to 0.999. The sole exception was relative delta in the frontotemporal derivations, with left and right correlations respectively of 0.881 and 0.888. This probably reflects the effects of slow horizontal eye movements, causing artifacts in the 1.5 to 3.5 Hz delta band smaller than the threshold levels set by the computer. For the LD subjects (col. B), the correlations ranged from 0.928 to 0.999. The sole exception was relative delta in the right frontotemporal, with a value of 0.903.

With some exceptions, the correlations between coherence or power asymmetry values from unedited and edited EEG samples were well above 0.900. Seven of the ten exceptions came from the frontotemporal derivations. Thus, visual editing caused few changes in neurometric EEG measures, except for data from frontotemporal derivations. Even these were not drastically altered. This suggests that differences in criteria for visual editing in different laboratories should not cause large variance in neurometric measures gathered with these methods.

It has been suggested by other workers that as few as 8 seconds of EEG will provide a reliable estimate of spectral density. It has been our practice to require that at least 20 seconds of EEG remain after visual editing in order to accept the numerical results emerging from the spectral analysis. Does the reduction of EEG data from approximately 60 seconds of machine-artifacted data to about 20 seconds of machine-plus-visual artifacting alter the correlation of edited to unedited record? The values of an independent comparison of twenty normal and twenty LD children is presented in columns C and D of table 2. The correlations between measures extracted from visually edited and unedited samples remain essentially identical to those of the previous study in which an average of 42.36 seconds of visually edited record were compared to nearly 60 seconds of unedited record. Thus, we concluded that using 20 seconds of record provides as adequate a sample for spectral analysis as a section twice as long. Finally, one might ask the question, "What constitutes a minimally acceptable length of computer-only artifacted record?" Column E of table 2 shows the correlation of 24 seconds of visually edited and 22 seconds of unedited record. Again, all correlations are highly significant.

In conclusion, it is our opinion that about 20 seconds of computer-artifacted record yields spectral estimates that are representative of those obtained from larger records. These data provide adequate reassurance that spectral estimates extracted from the records of children with varying amounts of artifact-free EEG (above a minimum of 20 seconds) can be legitimately compared.

Test-Retest Reliability

In order to evaluate the test-retest reliability of the measures extracted from the EEG in which several independent samples were examined within and between sessions, data were gathered from twenty-three normal children consisting of a sample of one minute of eyes-open and one minute of eyes-closed, computer-artifacted EEG at the beginning of the test session and after administration of the full neurometric battery one and one-quarter to two and one-half hours later. Data were first subjected to careful visual editing. Quantitative analyses were then performed on data from the beginning of the test session, when subjects were alert and perhaps tense, and from the end of the session, when subjects might be expected to be bored, possibly slightly drowsy, and certainly at ease in the situation.

In general, data obtained in the eyes-open condition were significantly less reliable than in the eyes-closed condition, and absolute power measures were found to be less reliable than relative power measures. We concluded that relative power measures from an eyes-closed EEG sample taken at the beginning of the session provided the most accurate indices of the structural and functional integrity and maturational development of the brain and focused on these EEG measures in our subsequent work.

Table 4 presents the correlation coefficients between the replicated sets of measures of relative power in the delta (1.5–3.5 Hz), theta (3.5–7.0 Hz), alpha (7–13 Hz), and beta (13–19 Hz) bands in the eyes-closed EEG samples taken at the beginning and the end of the recording session. All values in the table are significant at the .001 level or better, as assessed by Fischer's Z. Note that estimates of relative alpha are especially reliable. Estimates of posterior slow waves, particularly important because of the high incidence of excessive values in LD children, are also quite reliable. Values of delta and beta in the central regions are least reliable, but are still within an acceptable range. With the purpose of replicating and extending the test-retest reliability, three additional samples were gathered. First, a sample of fifteen neurologically impaired children was obtained from whom two within-session EEGs were taken; second, a group of thirty LD children who had a test and retest within a year (average interval 0.62 years); and third, a group of thirty LD children who were retested from two to three and one-half years following initial evaluation. Table 5 shows the test-retest correlations for all three groups. All correlations are significant at at least the .05 level, with the majority above the .01 level. For table 5 (which shows only the bipolar derivations for the left side of the head), the left set of columns represents a transformation of the age-related Z scores, while the right set of columns represents relative power that changes with age. All in all, the correlation holds up remarkably well over relatively long periods. These results have been confirmed by Fein et al. (1983, 1984) and Gasser et al. (1982).

Regression Equations for EEG Spectral Descriptors

In 1973, Matousek and Petersen published normative data on the average values and standard deviations of the absolute power in delta, theta, alpha, and beta bands for the eyes-closed EEG from eight bilaterally averaged bipolar derivations (F_7T_3/

F_8T_4, T_3T_5/T_4T_6, C_3C_z/C_4C_z, P_3O_1/P_4O_2) in a sample of 561 normal Swedish male children with uneventful developmental histories. Their normative data were calculated separately for cross-sectional age groups of 18 to 49 children at yearly intervals from one to twenty-one years of age. These data were transformed by us to relative (percent) power in each band and then further transformed by log $X/(100 - X)$ to achieve Guassianity. The accuracy with which this transform yields a normal (Gaussian) distribution has been confirmed by Gasser, Bacher, and Mocks (1982). Regression equations were computed for each measure separately for each derivation. Fourth-degree polynomial functions yielded a satisfactory fit for all measures, giving a substantial reduction in the estimated variance.

For each frequency band (delta, theta, alpha, beta) in each of the four bilateral pairs of derivations (frontotemporal, temporal, central, parieto-occipital), this procedure yielded a fourth-degree polynomial of the form:

$$\% \text{ Power} = C_0 + C_1^t + C_2^{t2} + C_3^{t3} + C_4^{t4}$$

Tables 6 and 7 present the values of the five coefficients C_0, C_1, C_2, C_3, and C_4 for each of the sixteen polynomial functions resulting from this procedure without (table 6) or with (table 7) log transformation. Since these are continuous functions of t (age in years minus 1.0), the value of each of the four spectral estimators, or of its log transform, in any of the eight bipolar derivations can be predicted simply by entering the chronological age of the subject into the appropriate equation. We routinely used age at the time of neurometric examination for this purpose, calculating age to two decimal places. Standard deviations are presented in table 8.

It should be noted that in later stages of the historical progression that we are narrating, these initial equations were first replaced by others based upon a larger sample of healthy U.S. children (John et al. 1980) and then extended to monopolar derivations and substantially expanded to include a large number of multivariate features (John et al. 1983; John, Prichep, and Easton 1987).

Accuracy of Prediction of EEG Features by Polynomial Functions

Next, we confirmed that a sample of normal, healthy U.S. children, with no history of neurological disease or inadequate academic achievement, showed approximately Gaussian distributions on these log-transformed spectral estimators with variances relatively independent of age (John et al. 1980, 1983). Thereafter, we routinely Z-transformed relative power measures in the four frequency bands from the eight derivations using the appropriate mean values and standard deviations. (See chap. 3 for details.) The resulting Z values provide an estimate of the probability that such a value would be obtained by chance from the same derivation in healthy individuals the same age as the subject, effectively regressing age and derivation out of the measurement. Most of our findings will be presented in terms of Z values instead of or in addition to the actual values of the data. However, table 9 presents actual data values in order to assess the accuracy with which EEG spectral features are predicted by the polynomial functions.

For nine-year olds, table 9 presents the values of absolute power in the delta, theta, alpha, and beta frequency bands for the frontotemporal, temporal, central, and parieto-occipital derivations as published by Matoušek and Petersen, the values of these measures after transformation to relative power, the values as predicted by the fourth-order polynomial functions, and the values of relative power actually measured by us in a group of forty-four normal nine-year-old male children from New York City.

Inspection of table 9 reveals that the mean values obtained from the demographically diverse sample of forty-four normal New York City nine-year-old male children lie within one standard deviation from the values predicted by the polynomial functions derived from twenty-five normal Swedish nine-year-old male children, except for the values of beta in the central and parieto-occipital regions which tend to be lower in the New York data. Taking into consideration that our amplifiers have somewhat more flat frequency response, that we used digital filters while Matousek and Petersen used analog filters with less steep cutoff, and that our sample had greater genetic and demographic diversity, the correspondence between the two sets of data seems excellent.

Table 10 presents the mean and standard deviations for the values of coherence and power asymmetry in the delta, theta, alpha, and beta bands for homologous pairs of frontotemporal, temporal, central, and parieto-occipital derivations obtained by analyses of the same EEG samples used for table 9. An expanded set of normative data for these measures and a large number of additional features has been published elsewhere (John, Prichep, and Easton 1987).

Comparability of EEG Spectral Features in Children from Different Cultures

For further evaluation of the age regression equations for mean values and deviations of relative power and the coherence and power asymmetry normative data described above, one-minute samples of computer-artifacted, eyes-closed EEG were gathered from four samples of normal children, graphically plotted and visually edited for possible artifacts. The resulting artifact-free EEG segments were subjected to spectral analysis using digital filters for the delta, theta, alpha, and beta bands, for data from bilateral central, temporal, parieto-occipital, and frontotemporal derivations. Coherence and power asymmetry were also computed separately for each band in every derivation. The four groups were:

Group 1. 25 normal 7-to-13-year-old male children with a mean age of 10.4, half from the Harlem district of

central New York City and half from middle-class
suburban New York communities;
Group 2. 22 normal 6-to-16-year-old male children with a
mean age of 12.0 from the same two districts of
New York City;
Group 3. 52 normal male and female children aged 6 to 16
years old from largely working-class suburban communities in Suffolk County, 40 miles outside New
York City; and
Group 4. 41 normal male and female children aged 5 to 11
years old with a mean age of 8.5 from both urban
and rural areas of Barbados, with normal birth,
developmental, and school histories. (F. Ramsay,
G. Solimano, N. Galler, E. R. John, H. Ahn, S.
Lobel, E. Mason. These data were gathered in a
collaborative research project supported by the
Ford Foundation.)

Spectral measures from each group were Z-transformed relative to the means and standard deviations of the age regression
equations described above. These Z transforms were computed using the value of the polynomial functions calculated on
the basis of the actual age of each individual subject in the four
groups. Means and standard deviations for values of coherence
and power asymmetry for each band and every derivation were
computed again on Group 1, and used to corroborate the values shown in Table 10. The agreement was sufficiently close so
that the values in table 10 were then used to compute Z transforms for the same measures for all members of the four
groups.

Tables 11 and 12 show the distribution of Z values for every
neurometric feature extracted from the one-minute computer
artifacted and visually edited sample of eyes-closed EEG, for
Groups 1, 2, 3, and 4. Table 11 presents the data for spectral
power estimators, and table 12 the data for coherence and power
asymmetry. To facilitate comparisons between groups of differ-

ent sizes, the data have been recast in terms of the percentage of members of each group whose Z-transformed features deviated from the predicted mean value at less than the $p = .05$ level, between the .05 and .01 level, between the .01 and .001 level and at greater than the .001 level. "Positive" findings are represented by Z-values that are improbable in a sample of healthy children with no history of neurological disease or head injury who are performing at grade level in school, and are presented separately for p values less than or equal to .05 but greater than .01, less than or equal to .01 but greater than .001, and less than or equal to .001. *Since these data showed no consistent or significant differences between left and right side derivations for any of these neurometric measures, the data from the two sides of the brain have been combined to reduce the size of these tables.*

Inspection of these data leads to a number of extremely interesting conclusions. *First,* the twenty-five children of *Group 1* showed 90 false positives out of 1,800 measures or 5 percent significant at better than the .05 level, 18 (1 percent) false positives at better than the .01 level, and only 2 instances (0.10 percent) of a false positive at better than the .001 level. This constituted an independent replication of the data shown in tables 9 and 10, demonstrating that the polynomial functions accurately predict spectral estimators for relative power in the delta, theta, alpha, and beta frequency bands, and that the coherence and power asymmetry values for the four frequency bands in the four bilateral derivations studies are tightly distributed.

Second, for the twenty-two normal children of *Group 2,* 54 of 1,584 values (3.4 percent) were significant at better than the .05 level, whereas 79 false positives could be expected by chance. This finding demonstrated that the predictions of the polynomial functions were valid for two samples of different mean age (10.4 and 12.0 years) and that the coherence and power asymmetry values did not change drastically from age six to sixteen. The distributions of values for Groups 1 and 2 on every neurometric measure were compared using the chi-square statistic; these data showed that the distribution of almost all of these measures was not significantly different in these two groups of children.

Third, the fact that false positives for Groups 1 and 2 together were within the chance level demonstrates that the predictions of the polynomial functions and the normative data for coherence and power asymmetry for neurometric EEG features were *equally valid for normal children from two different cultural environments,* the Harlem district and the middle-class suburbs around New York City.

Fourth, for the fifty-two normal male and female six-to-sixteen-year olds of *Group 3,* 176 of 3,744 values (4.7 percent) were significant at better than the .05 level, while 187 false positives could be expected by chance. Sixty-two values (1.6 percent) exceeded the .01 level and 8 values (0.2 percent) exceeded the .001 level. Comparison of Groups 1 and 2 versus 3 on each measure were carried out using the chi-square statistic; no significant differences were found. These findings constituted a third independent replication of the accuracy of the normative data for coherence and power asymmetry and of the predicted spectral power values calculated from the polynomial functions, across a wide age range, encompassing school children from kindergarten to high school. They also established that the predicted neurometric EEG normative values were applicable to a demographically diverse group of normal male and female children across this wide age range who lived in a working-class region of Suffolk County, one hour outside of New York City.

Fifth, for the forty-one normal five-to-eleven-year-old male and female Barbadian children of *Group 4,* 129 of 2,952 values (4.4 percent) were significant at better than the .05 level, while 148 false positives could be expected by chance; 39 values (1.3 percent) were significant at better than the .01 level, and 4 (0.1 percent) at the .001 level. Group 1 plus 2 plus 3 were compared to Group 4 on every measure, using the chi-square statistic; again, there were no significant differences between the distributions of the Z values for these measures between healthy children in the United States and in Barbados. These findings constituted a fourth independent replication of the coherence and power asymmetry of the normative data and accuracy of the predicted values for spectral power calculated from the polynomial functions. They also established that the predicted neurometric EEG normative values were applicable to a sample of normal male and female children who lived in predominantly rural areas of a Caribbean island with a markedly different cultural environment.

Distribution of False Positives

Table 13 summarizes the incidence of false positives at three different significance levels for forty spectral power estimators and for the thirty-two coherence and asymmetry measures for the four different groups and for the total group of 140 normal children performing at grade level in school. Of these values, 449 (4.5 percent) showed false positives at or better than the .05 level, 132 (1.3 percent) showed false positives at better than the .01 level, and 17 (0.16 percent) showed false positives at better than the .001 level. These values are almost precisely what would be expected by chance sampling of EEG features with a Gaussian distribution in a healthy population. This finding validates the use of conventional parametric statistical procedures for analysis of such data.

Further examination of table 13 shows that the incidence of false positives in the total 5,600 computations of spectral power estimators was 171 (3.05 percent) at or better than the .05 level where 280 would be expected by chance, 39 (0.7 percent) at or better than the .01 level where 56 would be expected by chance, and 1 (0.02 percent) at the .001 level. Thus, the number of false positives in spectral power estimates was somewhat below the chance level. In comparison, the incidence of false positives in the total 4,480 computations of coherence and power asymmetry was 278 (6.2 percent) at or better than the .05 level where 224 would be expected by chance, 93 (2.1 percent) at or better than the .01 level where 45 would be expected by chance, and 16 (0.35 percent) at the .001 level where 4 would be expected by chance. Aberrant values of coherence or power asymmetry must be interpreted with more caution than required for spectral power estimators. Perhaps thresholds for significant deviations should be set higher. Nonetheless, *multiple* aberrant coherence or power asymmetry values in the same individual, especially at significance levels above .05, rarely occur in normal healthy children. Although the incidence of false positives was substantially higher than for the spectral power estimators and higher than the chance level, coherence and power asymmetry measures can still be of substantial utility for the evaluation of learning disabled children or persons with neurological diseases.

The specificity (true positive/false positives) of coherence and power asymmetry measures can probably also be increased by the greater precision that can be achieved by construction of polynomial functions that take the age of the subject into account. The evidence that the lateralization of function that occurs with maturation (Giannitrapani 1967) is accompanied by electrophysiological changes supports this view. Such age-regressed normative equations for these measures have been recently published (John, Prichep, and Easton 1987).

Comparison between Normal Female and Male Children

The original Swedish normative data from which we derived the polynomial functions were based upon male children. It is well established that the incidence of learning disabilities related to brain dysfunctions is much higher among boys than girls. Nonetheless, a substantial number of girls also suffer from learning disabilities. It seemed important to compare male and female children with respect to the EEG spectral power estimators, and explicitly establish whether there were any systematic and significant differences between normal boys and girls on these measures.

For this purpose, we selected two new samples of data from the large body of data that had been collected. These samples were matched with respect to age and ethnic composition, but were drawn randomly from the pool of data from normal children who had the characteristics required for these samples. We will call these children *Group 5*. One sample contained data from fourteen white and fourteen black normal male children, with an average age of 10.7 years (age range 8.3 to 15.4). The second sample contained data from fourteen white and fourteen black normal female children, with an average age of 10.0 years (age range 5.7 to 14.7).

Tables 14 and 15 present the incidence of Z-transformed spectral power estimators and measures of coherence and asymmetry significant at the .05 and the .01 level in the male and female groups. Inspection of these tables reveals that there was no single estimator on which the male and female groups differed significantly from one another nor from the groups described earlier. Thus, the polynomial functions do not have any significant bias with respect to sex differences. These results constitute an additional replication confirming the validity of our normative equations.

Comparison between Normal Black and White Children

In chapter 5, we will demonstrate the high sensitivity of EEG spectral power estimators to brain dysfunctions related to learning disabilities. In view of the ease and economy with which such measures can be gathered, their replicability, the low incidence of false positives, their potential utility as measures of maturation, and their sensitivity to brain dysfunctions, it seems possible that neurometric methods will gradually become incorporated into the set of assessment instruments used to evaluate children with learning problems. Decisions about educational strategies and goals appropriate for individual children will be partially influenced by the profiles of neurometric features.

Quite properly, many persons are greatly concerned about possible cultural biases in current assessment instruments. The comparison between different groups of normal children discussed above revealed no significant differences between white U.S. children and black children from Barbados. However, black U.S. children are culturally and ethnically different from black Barbadian children. Thus, it seemed important to make an explicit comparison between white and black normal U.S. children, with respect to spectral power estimators.

For this purpose, we recombined the samples of data used in the previous section to seek for sex differences in the EEG. We constructed a white and a black sample, each with data from twenty-eight normal children. Half the data in each sample came from boys and half from girls. The average age of the black children was 10 years (age range 5.9 to 15.4), and the average age of the white children was also 10 years (age range 6 to 15.4).

Tables 16 and 17 show the incidence of Z-transformed values significant at the .05 and .01 level, for each of the EEG spectral power estimators and each of the coherence and asymmetry measures in the two samples. Comparison of these data using the chi-square statistic revealed only one significant difference, namely, the incidence of excessive delta activity in the left central region. Since one would expect two measures out of forty to show significant differences at the .05 level purely by chance, we consider that no cultural or ethnic bias exists in EEG spectral power estimators as far as normal black and white U.S. children are concerned.

EEG Normative Data: Conclusions

This series of five independent replications evaluated the estimators for relative power in four frequency bands in eight derivations, derived from data about healthy normal Swedish children published by Matousek and Petersen (1973). These initial neurometric normative equations yielded an excellent prediction for the neurometric indices obtained from all of the groups of normal children that we studied. These polynomial functions provided an accurate description of the eyes-closed EEG of healthy, normal children across a wide age range, whether they lived in urban, suburban, or rural settings, came from middle-class or lower-income families, were boys or girls, were black or white, lived in the United States or in Barbados. These findings led us to collect additional data and to construct an expanded set of normative equations. We expected these equations to describe changes in a wide variety of features of the EEG characteristic of the normal development of the human brain, without cultural, socioeconomic, sex, or other biases. This possibility has been energetically explored in the extensive collaborative studies described in chapter 6.

CHAPTER 5

Sensitivity of EEG Measures to Brain Dysfunctions Related to Learning Disabilities

Comparison of Groups of Normal (N), Specifically Learning Disabled (SLD), and Learning Disabled (LD) Children

The data presented in chapter 4 showed that the automatic computer artifact rejection was quite accurate, although all data to be discussed have been visually as well as computer edited. The data further demonstrated that the neurometric spectral power estimators, coherence, and power asymmetry measures extracted from the eyes-closed EEG recording have good test-retest reliability, and they are distributed in a Gaussian manner. Finally, the predictions of spectral power estimators derived from the age-regression equations, as well as the normative data for coherence and power asymmetry, have high validity as shown by the fact that the incidence of false positives in five independent samples of normal children was below the level expected by chance.

Having established that these measures were stable, reliable, and valid, we next asked whether they were sensitive to brain dysfunctions in children with learning disabilities. In an initial study, the same neurometric EEG measures were extracted from one-minute samples of computer-artifacted, eyes-closed EEG recordings (with subsequent visual editing), gathered

from two groups of learning disabled (LD) children: *Group 6*
(SLD) consisted of fifty-eight male and female children from six
to sixteen years old with IQs above 85, most of whom were
attending their local school but performing at least two grades
below their appropriate level in language skills, arithmetic
skills, or both. *Group 7* (LD) consisted of fifty-five male and
female children from six to sixteen years old with IQs between
64 and 84, most of whom were attending a special school (James
E. Allen Learning Center, Dix Hill, New York) for children
unable to learn satisfactorily in their local schools.

The distributions of the Z values obtained for the neurometric EEG data from the ninety-nine normal children in
Groups 1, 2, and 3 (described in chap. 4) were compared to the
data from the SLD and LD groups in tables 18 and 19. In order
to explore whether SLD and LD children displayed differential
amounts of improbable (*abnormal*) neurometric findings on the
two hemispheres, tables 18 and 19 separately present data from
left and right side derivations.

Table 18 reveals that both the SLD and LD groups showed a
significantly higher incidence of positive findings than the normal group in 40 EEG spectral power estimators from the
frontotemporal, temporal, and parieto-occipital derivations.
The differences between the learning disabled and normal children on thirty-two EEG measures of coherence and power asymmetry were far less striking, as seen in table 19.

Table 20 summarizes the total distribution of Z values of the
forty EEG spectral power estimators across all leads, for the
normal, SLD, LD, and combined SLD plus LD groups. The
average normal child showed 1.34 positive findings at the .05
level or better, less than the two such values that would be
expected among forty measures by chance. The false positives
at the .05 level or better were 3.4 percent of the total distribution of measures. In contrast, both the SLD and LD groups
showed an average of 5.35 positive findings at the .05 level or
better, almost *triple* the number expected by chance. The num-

ber of positive findings at the .05 level or better was 13.4 percent of the total distribution of measures, four times higher than in the normal children.

Table 21 presents the chi-square estimates of the differences between the distributions of Z values for all neurometric features extracted from the eyes-closed EEG in normal, SLD, LD, and the combined SLD plus LD groups. The data are presented separately for each derivation and for each measure. The SLD group differed significantly from the normal group on nineteen out of forty spectral estimators. One significant difference was found on coherence measures. Significant differences between these two groups were found on three of the sixteen power asymmetry measures.

The LD group differed significantly from the normals on twenty-one out of forty spectral estimators. One significant difference in coherence and three in power asymmetry measures were found.

The combined SLD plus LD groups differed significantly from the normal group on twenty-two out of forty spectral estimators. Two significant differences were found in coherence measures, and two significant differences were found in power asymmetry measures.

The SLD, LD, and combined SLD plus LD groups all showed the greatest difference from normal spectral values in the parieto-occipital derivations, characterized by an excess of delta, theta, and combined delta plus theta power. This confirms the numerous reports in the literature of excessive posterior slow waves in many children with learning disabilities. In all three groups, a significant deficit of alpha activity was found in this region, because so much of the power in the EEG spectrum was at slow frequencies.

The regions showing the next most marked deviation from normal values in all three groups were the temporal derivations, which showed a significant excess of delta plus theta and of delta power alone, plus a tendency for excess beta. There was no significant excess of theta power. Alpha deficiencies were again significant. A similar pattern, but less significant, was found in the frontotemporal derivations.

The major difference between spectral estimators for the SLD and LD groups appeared to be in the central regions. The SLD group showed less abnormal values in this region than did the LD group. Frontotemporal values of delta and of power asymmetry in the delta and theta bands were also more deviant in the LD group.

Taking all three sets of chi-square evaluations into consideration, the SLD, LD, and combined SLD plus LD groups showed significant deviations from the group of normal children on the distributions of Z values for 17 out of 24 measures of excess delta plus theta power, 18 out of 24 measures of excess delta power, 6 out of 24 measures of excess theta power, 19 out of 24 measures of low alpha power, and 2 out of 24 measures of high beta power. A total of 62 out of 120 tests of spectral estimators showed significant differences for the learning disabled groups. Only 4 of 48 measures of coherence and 8 of 48 measures of power asymmetry were significantly different. Thus, it appears that although low coherence and abnormal power asymmetry were present in some members of the learning disabled group, excessive slow waves and deficient alpha activity were much more prevalent.

Independent Replication

Although the SLD group and LD group differed in the nature of their learning problems, both groups were composed of children with learning difficulties. The consistency of the patterns of significant differences found between each of these groups and the normal group lead us to consider these data as two independent replications, which confirm the sensitivity of neurometric EEG measures of brain dysfunctions in two separate samples of children with learning disabilities. The italicized entries in table 21 are those measures found significantly different from normal children in both of these groups of learning disabled children. Note that of the total of twenty-four measures on which these two groups differed from the normal group, eighteen were replicated in both groups. Abundant additional data on children with learning disabilities and neurological disorders were gathered by us after these initial studies. The results have been reported in detail elsewhere (Ahn et al. 1980; John et al. 1983) and, for that reason, will be only briefly summarized in the next chapter. In essence, those data confirm the high sensitivity and specificity of neurometric EEG features to brain dysfunctions found in a high proportion of children with learning disabilities.

CHAPTER 6

Neurometric and Behavioral Studies of Normal and At-Risk Children in Several Different Countries

This chapter reports the results of an international collaborative study of neurometric EEG features and their relation to a variety of factors. This study was previously reported at the conference of the International Academy for Research in Learning Disabilities in Crete, Greece, on 28 June–3 July 1987. The authors of that collaborative study were E. Roy John (New York University Medical Center, New York, and the Nathan S. Kline Institute, New York), L. S. Prichep (New York University Medical Center, New York, and the Nathan S. Kline Institute, New York), Thalia Harmony (Universidad Nacional Autónoma de Mexico), Alfredo Alvarez (Centro Nacional de Investigaciones Científicas de Cuba), Roberto Pascual (Centro Nacional de Investigaciones Científicas de Cuba), Alexis Ramos (Universidad Centro de Venezuela), Erzsebet Marosi (Universidad Nacional Autónoma de Mexico), Ana E. Diaz de Leon (Universidad Autónoma del Estado de Mexico), Pedro Valdes (Centro Nacional de Investigaciones Científicas de Cuba), and Jacqueline Becker (Universidad Autónoma del Estado de Mexico). One way to validate the accuracy of inferences about the causes underlying a demonstrated learning disability is to formulate successful individualized prescriptive remediation. While some skillful clinicians achieve impressive levels of success in such endeavors, most remedial procedures target a group whose members display similar behavioral symptoms as if the underlying causes were homogeneous. Predictably, the outcome is unreliable. Some members of the group benefit and some do not, and the reasons for neither success nor failure become explicitly evident.

Another approach to inference of the causes underlying learning disability is to seek comprehensively for objective evidence of brain dysfunction in children with demonstrable behavioral deficits, to fractionate groups that display a homogeneously shared dysfunction into heterogeneous subgroups that display different patterns of apparent pathophysiology, and to validate the clinical significance of the physiological subtyping by demonstrating differential responses to various clinical interventions.

This second approach immediately confronts a major problem: no external criteria exist to validate any subtyping that might be achieved. If subgroups are identified, no individual prescriptive remediations exist ready for use after identification of the appropriate targets. Those who choose this approach encounter a paradox: the reference for any physiologically based system of differential diagnosis is the preexisting set of clinical neurological and neuropsychological diagnostic methods, which we suspect are neither accurate nor adequate.

In constructing the neurometric approach to analysis of the EEG, we elected to address the criterion problem by focusing first on the normal child. We asked whether the evolution of brain electrical activity in healthy, normally functioning children proceeded in a way that could be described quantitatively and objectively; that is, whether reliable *norms* could be established that encompassed the set of measurements derived from normal children. If such homogeneous developmental rules could be identified for normal children, possible deviations from such rules would then be sought for groups of children with cognitive dysfunctions. If such deviations occurred significantly more often in learning disabled children, it would become possible to search for subgroups sharing different pathophysiological profiles, thus revealing the heterogeneous substrates underlying similar behavioral deficits.

After fourteen years of work, the results of this endeavor, with respect to the EEG, can be summarized by a few major conclusions, which will be documented in the remainder of this chapter.

1. A large number of parameters of brain electrical activity can be described which change in an orderly way with the maturation of healthy, normally functioning children. These are referred to as *normative neurometric* features.
2. These developmental rules accurately describe the changes observed in the brain electrical activity of normal children in a variety of different cultures.
3. A high proportion of children with learning disabilities, neurological disorders, or a variety of antecedent risk factors display significant deviations from the normal distribution of these electrophysiological features.
4. Heterogeneous subgroups with different pathophysiological profiles can be identified within the population of children with learning disabilities.
5. Some of these subgroups have identifiable behavioral concomitants or respond differently to various treatments. Clinical correlates of other subgroups have not yet been identified, but are assumed to exist on a purely a priori basis.
6. Abnormal neurometric features are a *necessary but not sufficient* concomitant of many behavioral dysfunctions. To some extent, it appears that cultural factors such as stimulation may enable a child to compensate for neurological dysfunctions sustained as a result of antecedent risk factors. Alternatively, cognitive limitations not evinced in a school environment requiring only a low level of intellectual performance might become more evident in a more demanding environment. The enormous diversity of criteria for cognitive competence across cultures poses a severe problem for the identification of the normal child as well as the learning disabled child.

The neurometric analyses of the EEG were based upon a one-minute, artifact-free EEG sample. Recordings were made from the nineteen electrodes of the International 10/20 System (Jasper 1958), relative to linked ears. All data from collaborating institutions were collected using procedures and electronic equipment identical with those described by John (1977). Data analyses were carried out using the algorithms described by John et al. (1983), implemented in minicomputers or microprocessors programmed by each group. From each electrode, univariate quantitative features were extracted, reflecting the absolute and relative power in the delta (1.5–3.5 Hz), theta (3.5–7.5 Hz), alpha (7.5–12.5 Hz), and beta (12.5–25.0 Hz) frequency bands. Additional features were then computed to qualify the synchronization and symmetry in each of these four frequency bands between all pairs of electrodes located symmetrically on the head. The same set of features were also computed for the eight bipolar derivations used to collect the data described in chapters 4 and 5.

Certain aspects of the electrical activity in different brain regions are highly correlated, reflecting normal interactions between them. On one hand, treating such correlated features as independent can yield misleading statistical findings. On the other hand, many brain dysfunctions uncouple these relationships. For this reason, we have derived a large number of new *multivariate* features that define the normal interrelationships among sets of univariate features in terms of their covariance matrices. Deviations from the multidimensional norm are referred to as Mahalanobis distances (John et al. 1983, 1987). Incorporation of covariance data into neurometric assessments leads to a marked reduction in false positives and increased sensitivity to pathology, especially with subtle cognitive or psychiatric disorders (John et al. 1988).

An especially interesting application of these multivariate descriptors is the distinction between *maturational lag* and *functional deviation* (John et al. 1983). A maturational lag is defined as an abnormal Mahalanobis distance across some set of features that can be restored to the normal range by substituting an age different from the chronological age of the patient in the normative age-regression equations. In other words, the apparent physiological age of the patient is not the same as the patient's actual age. In contrast, a functional deviation is defined as an abnormal Mahalanobis distance that remains abnormal no matter what age is entered into the age regression equations. The observed profile would not be normal at any age.

These methods have been used to evaluate thirteen samples of children in five different countries: Barbados, Cuba, Mexico, the United States, and Venezuela (Harmony et al. 1987). These samples contained a total of 2,048 children.

Group 1. Normal American children (n = 306), ages 6 to 16.
Group 2. Normal Barbadian children (n = 129), ages 7 to 12.
Group 3. Normal Cuban children (n = 256), ages 5 to 12.
Group 4. Normal Mexican children, middle class (n = 28), ages 7 to 12.
Group 5. Normal Venezuelan children, middle class (n = 26), ages 7 to 12.
Group 6. SLD American children, IQ above 85, WRAT below 90 in arithmetic, language skills, or both (n = 159), ages 7 to 16.
Group 7. LD American children, IQ between 65 and 84, WRAT below 90 in arithmetic, language, or both (n = 143), ages 7 to 16.
Group 8. Neurologically at-risk American children (n = 533), ages 6 to 16.
Group 9. Mildly retarded Cuban children, IQ between 50 and 70 (n = 127), ages 5 to 12.
Group 10. At-risk Mexican children, antecedent events, cultural/SES disadvantaged, IQ 90 or above (n = 28), ages 7 to 12.
Group 11. At-risk Mexican children, antecedent events, low SES, IQ 90 or above (n = 30) ages 7 to 12.

Group 12. At-risk Venezuelan children, antecedent events, low SES, IQ 90 or above (*n* = 55), ages 4 to 12.

Group 13. Normal and at-risk rural Mexican children, low SES (*n* = 228), ages 6 to 16.

The criteria for normality, learning disability, or risk were basically similar in all of these studies and included medical history, academic records, WISC or Wechsler Preschool and Primary Scale of Intelligence (WPPSI) and WRAT or similar achievement tests, and a neurological examination except for Group 1.

Results

U.S.-Swedish Developmental Equations

In 1980, we published data (John et al. 1980) showing that the age-regression equations that we derived from 306 normal U.S. children in Group 1 closely corresponded to those that we extracted from data published for a large group of normal Swedish children (Matousek and Petersen 1973). The slopes of the equations describing normal black and white U.S. children were identical with those for the Swedish children.

Sensitivity of Neurometric Developmental Equations

Using the means and standard deviations of these neurometric equations, Ahn et al. (1980) compared the incidence of positive findings in U.S. normals, Barbados normals, and U.S. SLD, LD, and neurologically at-risk groups. False positives in the Barbados normals were below the chance level, while the incidence of positive findings in single features among the 32 univariate features studied were as high as 35 percent for the SLDs, 39 percent for LDs, and 47 percent for neurologically at-risk patients. The most common finding in the SLD and LD groups was an increase in delta and theta and a decrease in alpha activity in posterior regions. This finding is in agreement with a large number of similar reports using both conventional and computerized EEG evaluation (Hughes 1985; John 1977; John et al. 1983).

Independent Replications of Neurometric Norms

Since 1980, the accuracy of our neurometric developmental norms has been evaluated in studies published by teams in the United States (Yingling et al. 1986), Cuba (Alvarez, Pascual, and Valdes 1987), Mexico (Harmony et al. 1987), and Venezuela (Ramos cited in Harmony et al. 1987). In each study, the conclusion was "the normative values published by John et al. (1980) are an appropriate benchmark against which to assess learning disabled or other patient groups . . ." (Yingling et al. 1986). The agreement between our norms and data from the United States, Sweden, Barbados, Cuba, Mexico, and Venezuela indicate that these developmental rules describe the evolution of brain electrical activity in a way that is characteristic of healthy children from any ethnic background. We believe all healthy human brains develop according to the same rules. Racial differences do not exist.

Independent Replications of Sensitivity

Since 1980, the sensitivity of our neurometric equations to subtle brain dysfunctions has been evaluated in six independent studies (Ahn et al. 1980; Ramos in Harmony et al. 1987; Harmony et al. 1987; Alvarez, Pascual, and Valdes 1987; Yingling et al. 1986; Gasser et al. 1983). In five of these six studies, a high incidence of positive findings has been obtained in samples of learning disabled or at-risk children. In all of the five confirmatory studies, increased posterior slow waves were a common finding. The sole exception is the "neurologically pure" group of dyslexics studied by Yingling et al. (1986). The reasons for this contradiction are not clear, but it may be due to the more rigorous exclusion of children with soft neurological signs or risk factors from the sample under study.

Sensitivity of Maturational Lag

Alvarez, Pascual, and Valdes (1987) used the single multivariate neurometric feature "Maturational Lag" to classify normal versus mildly mentally retarded (MR) Cuban children. They achieved an accuracy of independent replication of 2.5 percent false positives and 81 percent correct positive findings. The results of these various studies of normal children, and of related studies of dysfunctional groups, are presented in table 22.

Interaction of Cultural with Risk Factors

A particularly interesting study on the contribution of cultural factors to brain compensatory mechanisms has been carried out (Harmony et al. 1987; Harmony 1988). Intrigued by the low incidence of school failure among members of Groups 10 and 11, in spite of numerous neurometric abnormalities, these authors noted that schools in marginal areas serving families with low cultural and SES levels placed low demands on children and questioned the validity of conclusions about learning disabilities drawn from schools with diverse criteria.

Accordingly, these workers studied the maturation of the EEG in 228 children in a small rural community called Tlaltizipan, about 50 kilometers outside Mexico City in the state of Morelos. These children were members of a cohort that has been evaluated at regular intervals from birth until present, by Dr. Joaquin Cravioto, FIARLD, of the Mexican Institute of Family Development. Their age range was from 6.5 to 15.5 years. All children attended the same school. The community under study is characterized by extensive poverty and extremely high levels of environmental pollution. In all of these children, risk factors were evaluated by examining personal and family medical histories, anthropometric curves, incidence of head injuries or loss of consciousness, perinatal hypoxia, birth order, and behavioral milestones relating to language comprehension or expression. Using these criteria for risk, the sample was divided into four groups: (I) children at grade level; (II) children one grade level below appropriate for their age; (III) children who were regularly left back in school; (IV) children who were illiterate. Each group was subdivided into those with and without antecedent risk factors.

Neurometric abnormalities relative to our norms were more marked in posterior head regions, especially for slow activity in the delta and theta bands. The most important finding in this study was the relative incidence of maturational lag in the eight different subgroups.

Examination of table 23 shows that the incidence of significant maturational lag was far higher in children at-risk due to antecedent factors than those who were not, as would be expected. However, it was quite unexpected to find that in Group I, maturational lag was 6 percent more frequent in children with antecedents than those without, in Group II the difference was 10 percent, in Group III it was 26 percent, and in Group IV it was 33 percent. The total incidence of abnormalities was similarly graded.

Since all of these children attended the same school and lived in similar circumstances of pervasive high risk due to poverty and pollution, the striking differences in the high risk members of each group in the incidence of neurometric abnormalities, summarized by the multivariate index of maturational lag, are reasonably attributable to family environment and stimulation. Since the economic circumstances in this community are quite homogeneous, children who fail regularly in school or remain illiterate are likely to come from uncaring parents. These findings raise the intriguing possibility that neither antecedent risk nor neurometric abnormality are necessary and sufficient for learning disabilities, but can be compensated for by stimulation. The data also suggest that some of the consequences of risk factors, such as poverty and pollution, on brain maturation may be prevented by a supportive environment and stimulation.

CHAPTER 7

Evaluation of Differences in EP Waveshapes between Normal and Learning Disabled Children

The full NB consists of 115 conditions and challenges derived from conditions. The results presented in chapters 4–6 come only from analysis of the one-minute sample of eyes-closed EEG at the beginning of the recording session. The 29 other NB items that assess the EEG under different conditions will be discussed elsewhere. The next chapters present results obtained from the 85 EP items of the full NB.

The data from every EP item were first analyzed by examining the significant differences between waveshapes averaged across samples of normal and learning disabled children from whom such data had been obtained. Inspection of the full body of such data revealed certain systematic differences that emerged across items. These systematic differences emphasized the need for a more quantitative description of EP morphology. This led us to develop the global or "multivariate" EP morphology descriptor discussed in chapter 8.

Using the t-test to evaluate the significance of differences between EPs averaged across groups of normal versus learning disabled children, and using the morphology descriptor to classify EPs from individual children in each group as normal or abnormal, we estimated the possible diagnostic utility of the waveshape obtained from every lead in the International 10/20 System in response to every EP item in the NB.

In additional samples of normal and learning disabled children subjected to only the core NB, we further evaluated the diagnostic utility of the multivariate morphology descriptor and a number of other quantitative "univariate" descriptors of potentially discriminating features extracted from the EP waveshapes. First, normative data consisting of the mean values and standard deviations of each of these features were determined for each EP item in the core NB for every electrode position, using a group of 122 normal children from six to fifteen years old. Then, in additional groups of normal and learning disabled children, the values of each of these features for each EP item were extracted, age-regressed, and Z-transformed relative to the appropriate normative data for every electrode. The distributions of values of these Z-transformed features were then compared in the groups of normal and LD children.

Grand Average EPs, Difference Waves, and T-Tests

Since the full NB contains eighty-five EP items, each producing a waveshape for every electrode in the 10/20 system, a total of 1,615 EP waveshapes would be yielded by the full examination of one individual. Our initial problem was to devise a strategy to evaluate the possible diagnostic utility of the information contained in each of this large number of waveshapes. We were all too aware of the dangers inherent in assuming that the learning disabled group, or for that matter even the normal group, could be considered homogeneous. This heterogeneity made it impossible to find the *normal* EP or the *abnormal* EP that would characterize all members of either group.

Yet, as we have pointed out, the normal and LD children providing the data for each EP item were different from item to item. We decided to begin by ascertaining for each EP item whether differences in morphology were sufficiently consistent, given the unique composition of the two groups used to obtain data on that item, so that significant intergroup differences could be found. If any such differences were *consistent* across some subset of EP items, in *spite* of the changing composition of the test groups, this would suggest that those differences reflected salient ways in which normal and learning disabled children responded differently to multiple NB test items. Objective measures to quantify these sensitive EP features might then be developed. Analysis of EP waveshapes from a single individual, using these feature extractors, might reveal a great amount of heterogeneity within the learning disabled group, since the NB items and electrode positions that manifested abnormal EP features would vary from individual to individual. Underlying this approach is the assumption that only *a limited number of basic physiological mechanisms are responsible for the morphology of the EP* elicited by any NB item. Therefore, heterogeneity of EP morphology within the learning disabled population must arise from variations in the particular mechanisms that are dysfunctional in different anatomical loci, though the extent of the dysfunctions are not infinitely variable.

Accordingly, we constructed Grand Average EPs and variances for the group of normal and learning disabled children for whom data were available on each EP item, for every electrode. The difference wave, N-LD, representing the difference between these two Grand Averages at each latency point along the analysis epoch, was then constructed. Finally, we computed the t-test for the significance of the difference between the two Grand Averages, taking into consideration the variance within each group. Readers who are distressed by the problems of nonindependence between such t-tests at 10 millisecond intervals, and the probability of obtaining apparently significant results by chance in view of the enormous number (1,900) of t-tests computed for each NB condition, should be reassured that the findings reported here are indeed meaningful by examining their distribution across latency and their consistency within particular latency intervals in multiple NB conditions and challenges.

The logical first step in describing our results would be to present the Grand Average EPs, N-LD difference waveshapes, and the t-tests for the significance of these difference waves for every electrode for each item in the NB. Since this entails a prohibitive amount of data, we have selected for presentation only the waveshapes from those electrodes that displayed the most significant and consistent intergroup differences within each set of NB items. In a substantial amount of subjects to whom the full NB was initially administered, we found that electrical artifacts from the solenoid delivering the tap or from cross-talk between timing pulses and data in the cabling of DEDAAS sometimes contaminated the first 50 milliseconds of the EP. These capacitative artifacts were intermittent and were eventually eliminated by re-wiring the system. In order to allow us to make use of all the data recorded from these children without concern that very short latency portions of the EP might be contaminated by such intermittent artifacts, all EP waveshapes illustrated here have the first 80 milliseconds suppressed, unless specifically noted otherwise. Although all EPs were visually examined prior to Grand Average computation, to exclude obviously invalid data, this further routine precaution ensured that less obvious effects due to these intermittent artifacts did not influence our quantitative measures.

Perception of Temporal Order

The items intended to evaluate perception of temporal order were regular and random sequences of flashes, clicks, and taps. The stimuli from each of the three modalities were averaged separately in the two sequences, yielding EPs to regular flash, random flash, regular click, random click, regular tap, and random tap. Because of the unpredictability of the modality of the stimuli in the random sequence, a $P300$ component was expected in the responses to the random stimuli even though no task was imposed. In the regular sequence, no $P300$ component was expected. The further expectation, of course, was that in normal children, who monitor their environment alertly, $P300$ would be larger than in learning disabled children, who presumably perceive relationships between environmental events less acutely.

Typical waveshapes illustrating our results are presented in figures 2, 3, and 4 respectively for flash, click, and tap. In these and most of the subsequent figures, there are four rows of waveshapes. The first row gives Grand Average EPs across the total groups of normal subjects for whom data were obtained on these test items. The second row gives Grand Average EPs across the total group of LD subjects. The third row gives the N-LD difference waves obtained by subtracting the waveshape on row 2 from that on row 1. The fourth row gives the t-tests for the significance of the N-LD difference waves at every latency point, taking into account the variance of the two Grand Average EPs. Each column presents EPs from a different NB test item. In figures 2, 3, and 4, column 1 presents EPs from the regular condition, column 2 from the random condition, and column 3 from the challenge regular-random.

Inspection of these three figures reveals a consistent picture. Paradoxically, the regular stimuli elicited a large, late positive component in the normal group, sometimes even larger than did the random stimuli. This apparent paradox may be explained by the fact that the regular sequence was the first EP item in the NB, when the overall situation was still novel and unpredictable for the child. The random sequence occurred much later, and was the NB item used to achieve dishabituation after a monotonous habituation procedure. The effects of order are also reflected in the larger amplitude observed in early components of EPs elicited by the regular stimuli.

Figure 2 shows that, at lead O_1, there was a very significant difference between N and LD in amplitude of an early component at about 120 ms and in later positive components between 300–400 ms in response to regular flash (col. 1), also seen for the later components in response to random flash (col. 2). The challenge EP wave, seen in the third row of data, was obtained by subtracting the random from the regular EP for each group.

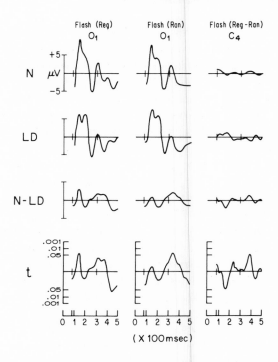

Fig. 2.   Prediction of temporal order (visual)

The challenge wave appears smaller because it represents the differences between those two responses and is always displayed at the same amplification. The most marked challenge EP for regular minus random flash was at lead C_4 (col. 3). This lead shows quite different challenge EPs for N and LD.

The normal group shows a significantly greater decrement than the learning disabled group in the positive component at 170 ms and in the positive-going process at 300–350 ms, when the regular and random items are compared. Thus, it seems that the normal group responds more vigorously to the initial NB items (regular) and shows greater late positive components in that EP than the learning disabled group. The normal group

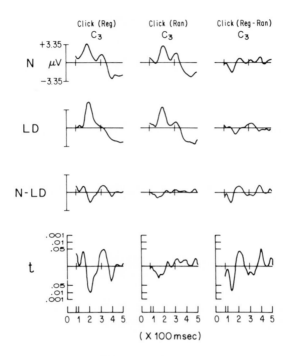

Fig. 3. Prediction of temporal order (auditory)

shows a greater decrement in the amplitude of the positive process at 170 ms to the subsequent NB item (random), while retaining greater positive components in the 300–400 ms latency region. This confirms our expectation that $P300$ would be greater for N than LD, and suggests that normal children may show larger EP amplitudes to more stimuli and more rapid habituation than LD children.

Figure 3 presents comparable data for regular and random click, from lead C_3. The results are similar to flash, except that the LD group fails to show the $P300$ component to regular click but does show it to random click, while the N group displays a strong $P300$ to both items. Unexpectedly, the N-LD difference

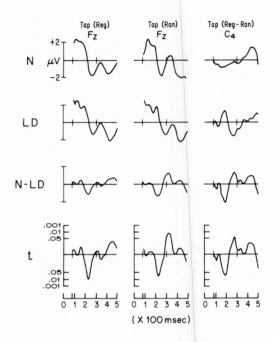

Fig. 4. Prediction of temporal order (somatosensory)

wave was far more significant for the regular than random click. Again, the regular novel random challenge EP was most marked in the central regions.

Figure 4 presents comparable data for regular and random tap, from lead F_z. As was the case with regular flash, the presentation of regular tap early in the test session elicited a clear $P300$ in both groups. The main difference between the two groups in response to regular tap is that the Ns show a larger negative amplitude at about 240 ms. However, more marked differences become apparent in response to random tap. The normal group continues to show a large negative wave at 240 ms, with a somewhat larger $P300$ than the response to regular tap. The LDs show a marked *latency shift,* with the large negative wave occurring 30–40 ms later and with the late positive component smaller and similarly delayed with respect to the normals. These differences are highly significant. No such latency differences between the two groups were found with regular or random flashes or clicks.

As in the previous flash and click challenges, the most marked challenge EP for regular minus random tap was observed in the central regions. Note the basic similarity of the N-LD difference wave and the t-test wave for the regular minus random challenge EPs in the central leads in figures 2–4. This suggests that the central regions may be implicated in the prediction of temporal order *independent* of the sensory modality of the predicted stimuli. Evaluation of this first set of NB conditions and challenges shows that construction of the challenge EPs unmasked an interesting process in which the central regions seem to participate quite differently in N and LD children, which could not readily be observed by examination of EPs to regular or random stimuli alone in any single modality.

Habituation and Rehabituation

Habituation was studied by computing the EPs to each of a series of five compound stimuli (simultaneous flash plus click plus tap) repeated at regular intervals. Decrements in EP components elicited by later compared with earlier stimuli within the series reveal short-term, or *phasic*, habituation. After repetition of a habituation sequence of twenty-five series, each of five stimuli, dishabituation was accomplished by presentation of a long sequence of randomly mixed flashes, clicks, or taps at random intervals.

Upon completion of the dishabituation procedure, rehabituation was studied by computing the EPs to each of a series of five compound stimuli, exactly as in the initial habituation procedure. If dishabituation occurred, indicating that the subject inhibited meaningless afferent input but continued to monitor that sensory modality for possibly meaningful change, the initial responses to the rehabituation stimuli *after* dishabituation would be expected to be larger than the final responses to the habituation stimuli *before* dishabituation. Further, if memory of the initial habituation procedure persisted after dishabituation, subsequent rehabituation should show a more rapid response decrement than the initial habituation effects. This would reveal long-term, or *tonic,* habituation.

The obvious expectations as to probable differences between groups of normal and learning disabled children on these procedures are that learning disabled children would show smaller EP decrements during habituation, less response increment after dishabituation, and less difference between initial habituation and rehabituation.

Figure 5 shows the EPs obtained by summing all the initial (H_1), second (H_2), third (H_3), fourth (H_4), and last (H_5) compound stimuli across the initial sequence of twenty-five series, each of five stimuli. The EPs presented were recorded from lead C_4, which showed the most significant N-LD differences in this procedure.

Both N and LD groups show very rapid phasic habituation, with approximately equal decrements in *peak to peak* amplitude that become asymptotic by the second compound stimulus in the series (18 to 12 μV for the normal group and 17 to 11 μV for the learning disabled group). Similarly rapid decrement was found in normal subjects by Fruhstorfer, Soveri, and Jarvilehto (1970), using this procedure, but with only a click stimulus. The N-LD difference wave showed a consistent peak at about 200 ms, which was highly significant for all five stimuli in the series. This reflected the presence of a complex, sustained negativity in the early part of the normal group EPs, while the EPs from the learning disabled group return rapidly to the baseline and swing positive about 50 ms before the normals.

Figure 6 shows the differences between EPs as a function of the position of the stimulus in the habituation series for lead P_3, which showed the most significant N-LD differences on these

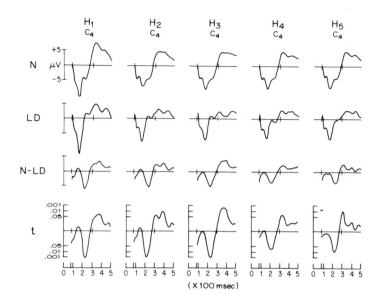

Fig. 5.   Habituation (flash + click + tap)

challenges. As expected from the fact that most of the amplitude decrement occurs by the second stimulus in the series,
these challenge EPs are of approximately constant size. The
major reason for the very significant intergroup differences on
these challenges is the large second negative wave at 240 ms in
the normal group which is almost completely absent in the learning disabled group.

Figure 7 shows the EPs obtained by summing all the initial
(R_1), second (R_2), third (R_3), fourth (R_4), and last (R_5) compound stimuli across the rehabituation sequence of twenty-five
series, again recorded from lead C_4, which showed the most
significant N-LD differences in this procedure.

Both the N and LD groups showed slight dishabituation.
Their initial responses to R_1 were, respectively, 14 and 11 μV in
peak-to-peak amplitude, compared with 13 and 10 μV for H_5 at

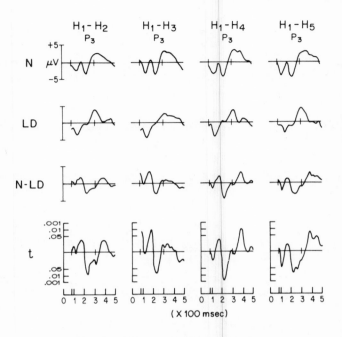

Fig. 6.   Changes during habituation

the end of habituation. Rehabituation proceeded quickly in both groups. The mean amplitude of the EP in the normal group drops from 14 (R_1) to 11 (R_2 and R_3) to 9 μV (R_4 and R_5), while in the LDs the corresponding decrements are, surprisingly, relatively larger and more rapid, i.e., 11, 6.5, 6.5, 7.0, and 6.0 μV. Thus, rehabituation proceeded rapidly in both groups but may have been accomplished at a slightly greater and faster overall decrement in the LDs.

The N-LD difference waves and t-tests shown in figure 7 for rehabituation are almost identical with those shown in figure 5 for habituation. The major components contributing to these waves are once more the early negative process that persists until 250 ms in the normals but ends by 200 ms in the LDs. The

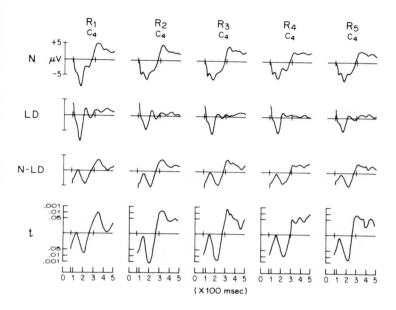

Fig. 7.   Rehabituation (flash + click + tap)

LDs also show a markedly smaller late positive complex than
the normals.

Figure 8 shows the differences between EPs as a function of
the position of the stimulus in the rehabituation series for lead
T_5, which showed the most marked intergroup differences on
these challenges. Reflecting the rapidity of rehabituation, these
challenge EPs are of approximately constant size within each
group. The major source of the highly significant N-LD differences on these challenges is the appearance of a second negative
wave at about 240 ms in the challenge EP of the normal group,
which is absent in the LDs. This second negative wave closely
resembles that shown in figure 6 for lead P_3, and suggests that
this process is quite widely distributed. There are also later
significant features of the N-LD wave, reflecting the virtually

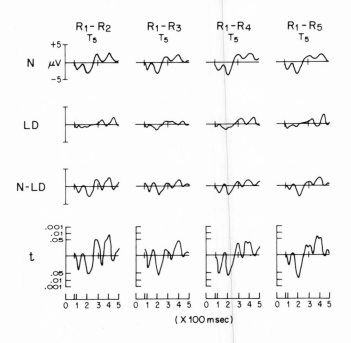

Fig. 8.   Changes during rehabituation

complete disappearance of late positive components of the EP in the LD group during rehabituation.

The memory or persistence of initial habituation is reflected by the differences between corresponding elements in the habituation and rehabituation sequences. Such effects reflect tonic habituation. The differences between the N and LD groups on these challenge EPs was seen most markedly at lead T_6, illustrated in figure 9. Again, the salient feature of the N-LD wave responsible for these significant differences was a negative wave at 240 ms, which was essentially absent in the LD group.

Thus, the data show that the normal and learning disabled groups differed little with respect to the relative changes in amplitude produced in the EP during habituation, dishabit-

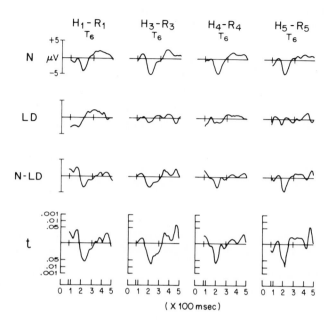

Fig. 9.   Memory of habituation

uation, and rehabituation. Phasic habituation proceeded with
equal rapidity in both groups of children. However, tonic habituation, measured as the memory of habituation, was more
marked in the normal group. This suggests that the mesencephalic reticular formation, shown to mediate tonic habituation
by Sharpless and Jasper (1956), may be underactive in a high
proportion of the LD children. Significant waveshape differences between the two groups were found in every challenge
and condition relating to these procedures. These N-LD differences were consistently maximal for a negative wave at 240 ms,
most clearly observed in different leads for the various test
items. Taken together, this set of data suggests that activation of
the reticular formation contributes to a negative EP component
with a peak latency about 240 ms.

Effects of Changes in Visual Contrast
(Items 62–66)

The intended purpose of presenting visual stimuli equated for intensity but with different degrees of contrast was to obtain an objective estimate of visual acuity, without which some of the subsequent EP items could not be interpreted without ambiguity. Accordingly, we selected three different 50 percent transmission grids: 65 lines per inch, presented out of focus and seen as a blank flash; 7 lines per inch, seen as a grid by any person with better than 20/200 vision; and 27 lines per inch, seen as a grid by any person with 20/20 vision. Since appearance of contrast in a previously blank field is known to change the visual EP waveshape in occipital leads O_1 and O_2 between 110 and 150 ms latency, two acuity challenges were available by subtracting the EPs elicited by the 7 lines per inch or 27 lines per inch stimulus from the EP elicited by the blank flash. By using the t-test to evaluate the significance of the challenge EP between 110 and 150 ms, visual acuity could be assessed objectively.

The literature on effects of changes in visual contrast on the EP waveshape of which we were aware was confined to observations from O_1 and O_2. As soon as we began to record EPs from these test items, we realized that in normal children, most leads in the 10/20 system showed definite changes in EP waveshape if such changes occurred in the primary sensory regions for vision, O_1 and O_2. Thus, it appeared that one might use the effects of changes in visual contrast to assess the transmission of elementary information about the content of the visual field from primary sensory cortex to other cortical areas. Many defects in information processing might depend upon a physiological operation, such as transmission, independent of the content of the operation. From this viewpoint, the absence of significant changes in EP waveshapes in other regions of cortex, despite O_1 and O_2 changes indicating adequate acuity to resolve the patterned stimulus, might reveal local information processing defects related to learning disabilities.

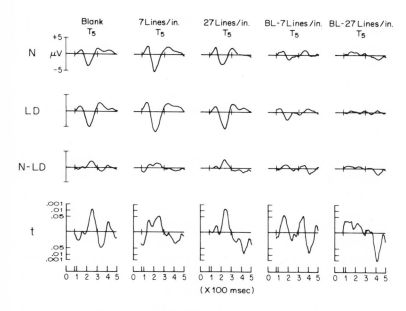

Fig. 10.   Effects of changes in visual contrast

Figure 10 illustrates the effects of changes in visual contrast on EPs from lead T_5, which showed the most significant differences between the N and LD groups. For blank, 7 lines per inch, and 27 lines per inch, the N-LD difference waves show highly significant differences between the two groups. Examination of the Grand Average EPs for the two groups reveals a negative component at about 220 ms, that is consistently 2 to 4 μV larger and 10 to 30 ms later in the EP from the LD than from the normal group, with the 27 line-per-inch stimulus eliciting the largest amplitude and latency difference between the two groups. *This effect is particularly noteworthy in view of the fact that at that latency, little or no difference between the two groups was elicited by a regular or random full field blank flash that was much brighter.* The positive wave, at about 300 ms in the normal group, was similarly delayed about 30 ms in the learning disabled group in response to the 27 line-per-inch stimulus. Surprisingly, the learning disabled group also showed a more vigorous response to coarse contrast (7 lines per inch) in the visual field, showing a significant N-LD difference at 150 ms to the blank minus 7 lines-per-inch challenge. No delay is apparent in this challenge EP when the two groups are compared. The significant difference evident between the two groups in the blank minus 7 lines-per-inch and 27 lines-per-inch challenges, at 450 ms, appears to be due to a late positive component displayed by the learning disabled but not the normal group.

Perception of Geometric Forms (Items 67–74)

In order to evaluate perceptual processes reflecting size and shape invariance but pertaining to innately different geometric forms rather than very similar symbols with different semantic meaning, we used large and small squares and diamonds as visual stimuli. EP differences elicited by stimuli of equal size and contrast but different shape should reflect geometric form perception, while similarities in EPs elicited by geometric forms of the same shape but different size would reflect size invariance. Intuitively, one expected members of the learning disabled group to show less distinction between forms of similar size but different shape and more distinction between forms of similar shape but different size, relative to the normal group.

Figure 11 compares the EP waveshapes to the four forms in lead P_3, where most significant differences were found between the two groups. For each test item, the most significant component in the N-LD difference wave is due to a negative process sustained until about 250 ms in the learning disabled group but giving way to a positive process at about 200 ms in the normal group. The maximum N-LD difference appears at about 240 ms in all four test items. This difference is similar to what was seen earlier in response to the compound stimuli used in habituation, but is opposite in sign.

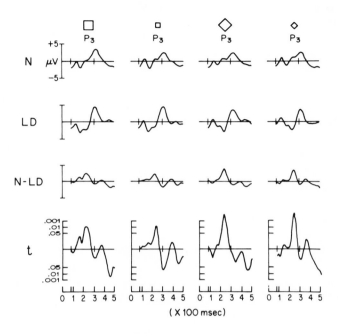

Fig. 11.   Perception of geometric form

Figure 12 illustrates the challenge EPs elicited by comparing similar shapes of different sizes and different shapes of similar sizes in lead C_z or C_3, which displayed the most significant intergroup differences on these test items. Three of the four N-LD difference waves show the major significant component at 240 ms. The differences between EPs elicited in the two groups by similar shapes of different sizes is significant but difficult to interpret. The differences between EPs from the two groups elicited by similar shapes of different sizes is qualitative rather than quantitative. Nonetheless, some process at about 240 ms seems to behave very differently in the two groups of children. The differences between EPs elicited in the two groups by stimuli of different shapes but equal sizes is apparently due to the appearance of substantially larger differences in the normal

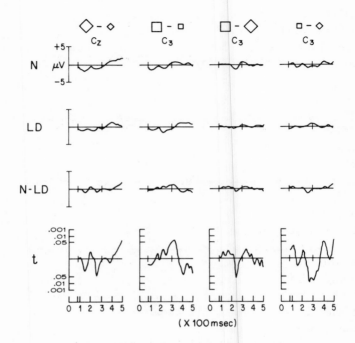

Fig. 12.   Shape and size invariance

than in the learning disabled group. These data suggest that in the left parietal brain region, normal children show more marked EP differences than learning disabled children between responses to two shapes of equal size but different form.

Letter Perception (Items 75–83)

In order to evaluate perceptual processes related to identification of letters of equal size and contrast but differing with respect to absolute orientation of critical features, we used the letters *b, d, p,* and *q.* These letters are the most frequently reversed by children with learning disabilities, and can be discriminated only by reference to some absolute criterion of asymmetry.

Figure 13 illustrates the EPs elicited by these test items in lead P_3, which displayed the most marked intergroup differences. Examination of these waveshapes shows quite impressive similarity in the EP response from letter to letter within each group, although small differences can be discerned. However, in each case the N-LD wave reveals the most significant difference in response of the two groups to be at about 240 ms, attributable to a component at that latency which is consistently negative in the LDs but positive in the normals. This same difference was seen just previously (fig. 11) in the items dealing with perception of geometric forms.

Figure 14 displays the challenge EPs reflecting the differences between EPs to the different letters in the two groups, for the central leads which showed the most consistent and significant intergroup differences on these challenges. For *b-d, p-q,* and *b-p,* the major differences are located at about 240 ms. In addition, for *b-d, d-q,* and *b-q,* significant differences are seen at 400 to 450 ms. Comparison of figures 13 and 14 with figures 11 and 12, which presented the results of assessing EP items related to shape and size variance, does not suggest that the processing of letters in these children activates mechanisms very different from those that mediate the evaluation of small geometric forms.

Figure-Ground Relations (Items 87–98)

In order to evaluate the structuring of figure-ground relations, both ipsi-modal and cross-modal, we presented regular sequences of flash, click, and tap, alone and in conjunction with meaningful auditory (music) or visual (video pictures) material. The hypothesis underlying these choices of NB items was that normal children were more likely to show quantitative decrease of response to irrelevant background events during input of competing meaningful material, while preserving the qualitative nature of the response to the meaningless background. In contrast, learning disabled children seemed more likely to show

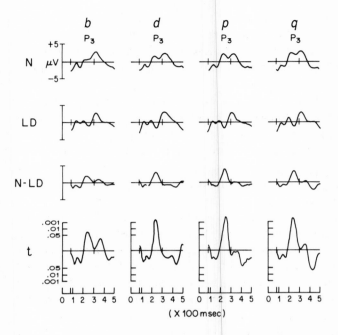

Fig. 13.   Letter perception

qualitative changes to the background stimuli, reflecting interaction with the meaningful input rather than quantitative attenuation reflecting inhibition of the meaningless background.

Figure 15 illustrates the interaction between ipsi-modal visual figure (video) and visual ground (flash), for the central leads where the most marked N-LD differences were found, and for lead O_1, where the challenge EPs were most different. The N and LD group waves show surprising qualitative similarities, with quantitative differences that are not striking, barely reaching the $p < .05$ level at 275, 240, and 350 ms in the three columns of data. Both N and LD groups show attenuation of EP amplitude to the meaningless flash in the presence of focused video, and both groups show qualitative changes in the EP, suggesting interaction of figure with ground as well as inhibition.

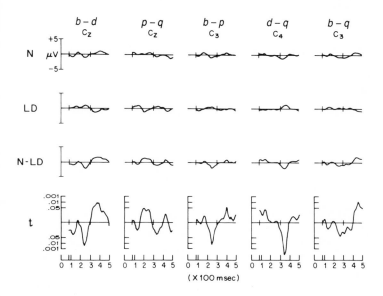

Fig. 14.   Differences in letter perception

Figure 16 illustrates the interaction between cross-modal visual figure (video) and auditory ground (click), for the central vertex leads where the intergroup differences were again most marked. Again, both groups show fundamental similarity of EP waveshapes to both test items. Both groups show attenuation of EP amplitude to the meaningless click in the presence of video, and minor qualitative changes in EP waveshape with respect to a positive component in the 300 ms latency domain. This may indicate nothing more than that the subject decreased prediction of click occurrence while attending to the video picture. The most significant component of the N-LD wave was at 240 ms for both test items, reflecting the longer persistence of the initial positive wave in the learning disabled group. The major difference between the challenge EPs for the two groups is also at 240 ms.

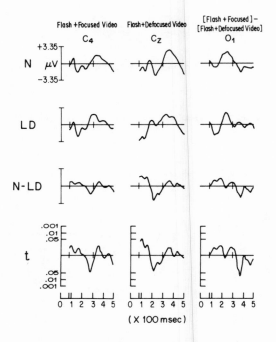

Fig. 15.　Figure-ground relations (video-visual)

Figure 17 illustrates the interaction between cross-modal visual figure (video) and somatosensory ground (tap), for lead F_z where the most marked intergroup differences were found. Both groups show attenuation of the amplitude of short latency components of the tap EP in the presence of video, but only slight indications of qualitative changes in EP waveshape. The major N-LD differences to the two test items consist of a much smaller initial positive wave in the learning disabled group, in the 80 to 100 ms domain, and smaller negative waves at 240 and 400 ms. The major difference in the challenge EPs is at 240 ms at lead F_7.

Figure 18 illustrates the interaction between cross-modal auditory figure (music) and visual ground (flash) for lead O_1, where the test items yielded the most marked intergroup differ-

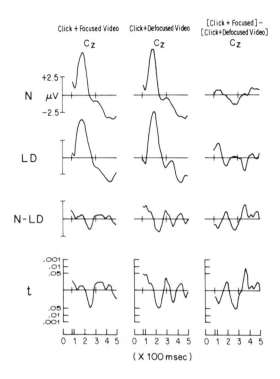

Fig. 16.   Figure-ground relations (video-auditory)

ences. Both groups show a quantitative reduction in amplitude of the flash EP during music but show only minor qualitative changes in waveshape. The learning disabled group shows a markedly smaller initial positive component, at about 120 ms, but also shows a second positive component peaking at about 200 ms that is absent in the normal EP. The challenge EP showed only minor differences, largest in lead T_6.

Figure 19 illustrates the interaction between ipsi-modal auditory figure (music) and auditory ground (click) for lead C_3, where the test items yielded the most marked intergroup differences. Both groups show a quantitative reduction in amplitude

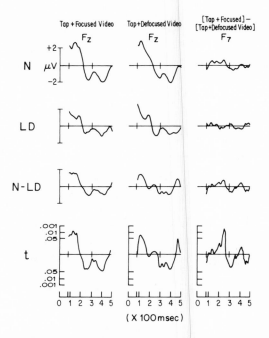

Fig. 17.   Figure-ground relations (video-somatosensory)

of the click EP during music. The normal group shows slight latency changes but basically similar EP morphology in the two conditions, but the LD group shows a definite qualitative change, resembling the normal group more during music than when listening to click alone. The major differences in the N-LD waves are at 220 to 240 ms and at 300 ms for both items. The major differences in the challenge EP were found at lead T_6, in the 250 and 300 ms latency regions.

Figure 20 illustrates the interaction between cross-modal auditory figure (music) and somatosensory ground (tap), for lead F_z, where the most marked intergroup differences were found. Both groups, but especially the normals, showed a quantitative reduction in the amplitude of the tap EP during music. Al-

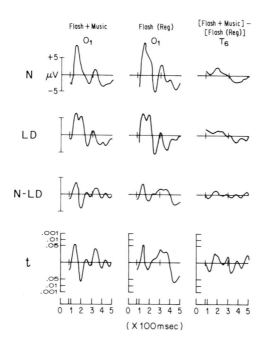

Fig. 18.   Figure-ground relations (music-visual)

though there were slight latency changes, neither group showed a qualitative change in waveshape. The major differences in the N-LD waves were at 240, 300, and 400 ms. The major differences in the challenge EP were again found at lead T_6, at 120, 240, and 300 ms.

In summary, both the N and LD groups showed quantitative reductions in EP amplitude in all cross-modal figure-ground interactions. During ipsi-modal interactions, qualitative changes were seen in both groups for visual input and in only the learning disabled group for auditory input. Thus, the results of figure-ground interactions corresponded to our expectations (i.e., that the two groups would display generically different effects) in only *one of the six conditions studied*. Although the expected effects

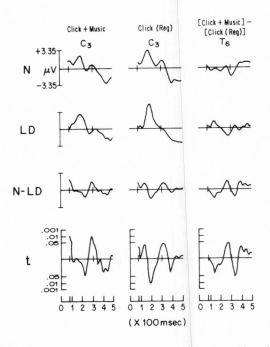

Fig. 19.   Figure-ground relations (music-auditory)

were not sufficiently strong to be reflected in the group Grand
Average EPs, due to their heterogeneous composition, other
evidence will be presented that suggests that strong qualitative
effects do occur in a substantial number of LD children. It may
also be worthwhile to point out that the most marked intergroup
differences for all auditory figure-ground challenge EPs were
found at lead T_6, suggesting an important role for this region in
integration of auditory with other types of information.

Sensory-Sensory Conditioning (Items 99–115)

The sensory-sensory conditioning test items were administered
to twenty-five normal children. In agreement with the litera-

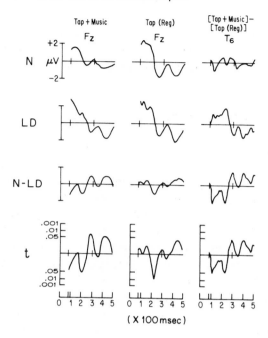

Fig. 20. Figure-ground relations (music-somatosensory)

ture, we found that the EP to the stimulus that was the conditioned stimulus (CS) became greater in the primary sensory region normally responsive to the unconditioned stimulus (US) after a period of CS-US pairing. Thus, flash produced a greater EP in central regions after pairing with click, and click produced a greater EP in occipital regions after pairing with flash. These effects were not due to pseudoconditioning, since tap EPs in these regions were unchanged by the flash-click or click-flash pairing.

Unfortunately, the procedure required for this sensory-sensory conditioning is lengthy and very tedious. We found that all but three of the LD children subjected to these test items were unwilling to permit the full set of measures to be obtained. It was not possible to obtain sufficient data to learn whether significant differences exist between normal and learning disabled groups. Thus, sensory-sensory conditioning is not a feasible measure to include in an electrophysiological test battery for learning disabled children.

Significant N-LD Differences on All EP Items

In the previous section, we presented illustrations of the Grand Average EPs for the N and LD groups, N-LD differences waves, and t-tests for the significance of those differences, for the leads at which the most marked and consistent intergroup differences were found on every EP condition and challenge. Repeatedly, marked differences appeared in certain latency domains, even though the lead displaying the clearest effects varied from item to item. Differences in the 240 ms latency domain were impressively consistent across a variety of NB items. In many instances, this was due to the fact that one group showed a longer initial positive deflection, moving negative more slowly than the other group. In a few instances, certain leads revealed a separate, relatively short negative process peaking at about 240 ms. The data suggested that this process sometimes occurs "appropriately" in the normal group, while failing to occur in the learning disabled group. In other instances, it occurs "inappropriately" in the LDs but is absent in the normals. Sometimes it appears to be superimposed on another component that partially masks it, appearing clearly only in the N-LD difference wave or in challenge EPs. Occasionally, components could be seen at latencies other than 240 ms in the Grand Average EP of one group that were absent from that of the other group. In addition, although we pointed out only those examples that were most striking, the learning disabled group often showed 10 to 30 ms latency delays for particular components that appeared earlier in EPs from the normal group that had basically similar morphology. Finally, the learning disabled group tended to show consistently smaller EP amplitudes than the normal group.

These various observations suggested that, in spite of the

heterogeneity of both the normal and the learning disabled group and the changing composition of the independent samples of individuals who comprised each group from item to item, a number of systematic differences existed between the two groups. These differences were repeatedly apparent no matter what the modality or context of the stimulus eliciting the EP. Since systematic differences in amplitude, latency, or presence of specific components existed between different independent groups of normal and learning disabled children across this diverse set of stimulus conditions, we reached the conclusion that it might be possible to define objective procedures to extract quantitative features from the EPs of individual subjects that would discriminate between normal and learning disabled children. However, all the information available from visual evaluation of the N-LD difference waves was certainly not represented by the selected examples that we have presented. For that purpose, it was necessary to catalog all the statistically significant differences between Grand Average EPs from the normal and learning disabled groups, indicating the latencies at which such differences were found, for each lead in the 10/20 system and for every EP item in the NB.

We constructed histograms showing, for every lead in the 10/20 system, the latencies at which any differences significant at the $p < .01$ level were found between the N and LD Grand Average EPs, for all NB items. Because they are so voluminous, we show here only the illustrative histograms for leads P_z, P_3, P_4, T_5, T_6, O_1, and O_2 for the items involving visual stimuli (table 24). Obviously, many such differences might be expected by chance, in view of the enormous number of t-tests that were computed (44 points, at 10 ms latency intervals from 80 to 520 ms in the analysis epoch, for each lead times 19 leads times 75 visual EP items equals 62,700 t-tests). The histograms were constructed for twenty-two 20 ms latency intervals (combining data from two latency points each) and for nineteen leads. Thus, an average of about one significant N-LD difference at the $p < .01$ level (or about five at the $p \le .05$ level) can be expected in any interval for any lead by chance $[627/(44 \times 19) = .75]$. If any latency interval for any lead contained more than five significant differences, this arbitrary level was considered a convincingly nonrandom finding.

Perhaps more intuitively convincing, significant differences due to chance should be randomly distributed across latency intervals within as well as between leads. The data from the full NB, administered for many items to groups comprised of differing individuals, can be considered as repeated, independent replications of similar measures. From this pragmatic viewpoint, inspection of the histograms makes it quite obvious that the observed significant intergroup differences are not reasonably attributable to chance.

In response to visual stimuli, across a variety of NB items, Fp_1 showed consistent intergroup differences in the 100–120 and 260–80 ms domains, while Fp_2 showed significant differences only between 260 and 280 ms. F_7 showed consistent differences in the 80–100 and 300–320 ms domains, while F_8 showed differences only in the 80–100 ms regions. F_3 showed significant differences in the 140–50 ms regions, while F_4 showed differences in the 80–120 ms domains. F_z showed significant differences in the 80–100 ms regions. Thus, frontopolar and frontal leads show most significant differences in response to visual stimuli relatively early, especially in the 80–120 ms domain (twenty out of thirty findings above the chance level).

Under these conditions, significant differences above the chance level appeared in anterior temporal leads in T_3 in the 260–80 and 320–40 ms domains and in T_4 in the 320–40 and 360–80 ms domains.

In central regions, significant differences appeared in C_3 in the 220–60, 300–320, 360–80, and 440–60 ms regions; in C_4, in the 200–220, 300–320, and 360–80 ms regions; in C_z, in the 200–220 and 300–320 ms regions. In the posterior temporal leads, significant differences were found in T_5 in the 220–60 ms domain and in T_6 in the 200–260 ms region. In parietal regions, significant differences appeared in P_3 in the 80–100, 240–60, and 320–40 ms domains; in P_4, in the 220–60 and 360–80 ms regions; and in P_z in the 80–100, 200–220, and 240–60 ms regions. In occipital regions, significant differences appeared in O_1 in the 80–100 and 240–60 ms domains; and in O_2, in the 80–100, 200–220, and 240–60 ms domains. (See table 24.)

Computations of the significance of N-LD differences at successive time points separated by 20 ms are obviously not independent. Our calculations about what actually constitutes the chance level assume such independence. In fact, it is probably just as valid to rely upon subjective judgment. Inspection of table 24 compels the realization that significant differences are clustered within certain latency bands in O_1, O_2, P_3, P_4, P_z, T_5, and T_6; while such differences are very unlikely in other latency intervals. Although anterior regions of the head show somewhat different effects, these too tend to be concentrated in certain intervals and unlikely in others.

Similar conclusions arose from inspection of the histograms for intergroup differences on auditory or somatosensory stimuli. These findings provided further evidence that the differences in EPs from independent groups of normal and learning disabled children were markedly consistent, in spite of the diverse stimulus conditions and the acknowledged heterogeneity of both the N and LD populations. Thus, appropriately defined feature extractors might yield quantitative indices that would discriminate between normal and learning disabled children.

CHAPTER 8

Quantitative Evaluation of Individual EP Morphology

Throughout the foregoing presentation of results, we have repeatedly expressed our belief that evaluation of the diagnostic utility of NB items by use of the t-test to assess the significance of N-LD differences in Grand Average EPs was inherently weak, because it could only reveal effects sufficiently robust to overcome the heterogeneous composition of both groups. Items that yielded even extremely bizarre responses from but a small proportion of the LD sample would be improperly discarded if these preliminary evaluations were accepted as conclusive. Further, the t-test for significant differences between EPs is a measure with an inherent limitation, because it is sensitive to large effects localized to restricted time domains but insensitive to smaller effects distributed across the whole analysis epoch.

In spite of these limitations, coarse screening of the huge volumes of data obtained from the EP items of the NB revealed impressively consistent phenomena. Numerous significant differences between the N and LD groups were found for many items in most leads. These differences were restricted to particular latency intervals independent of the nature of the stimuli. These findings made us believe that it would be useful to construct objective descriptors of such EP features as amplitude, signal-to-noise ratio, and symmetry, as well as a multivariate descriptor of EP morphology, for each of several specific latency regions.

Development of such quantitative EP feature extractors, together with measurement of their mean values and standard deviations in a large group of normal children, would enable us to take a critical step. We might thus move from the search for statistically significant differences between group Grand Average EPs, from which normal as well as abnormal individuals might deviate appreciably, to the classification of EPs from single individuals as normal or abnormal, on the basis of the established statistical distributions of normative feature extractor values. We call this the *neurometric* approach (John 1977; John et al. 1977a, 1983; John, Prichep, and Easton 1987).

Our first step in this direction was to try to develop a multivariate descriptor of overall EP morphology. The procedure followed has been described in detail in chapter 3 and is based upon principal component factor analysis of sets of EPs, which we have discussed elsewhere (John 1972, 1977; John et al. 1977a). Essentially, a sample of EPs from a large number (n) of normal children was obtained for every lead of the 10/20 system, for every EP item of the NB. Each such set of n EPs was subjected to factor analysis, yielding a set of K factor waveshapes. In practice, K is usually much smaller than n. The factor waveshapes can be considered as the dimensions of the *signal space* that contains the original EPs. This means that each of those EPs can be approximated, to within any specified error, by summation of appropriate amounts of each factor wave. We have found, for most leads and items, that four or five factors can usually account for more than 90 percent of the variance of a set of fifty normal EPs. The contribution of each factor F_j required for accurate reconstruction, varies for the EP from every lead i, EP_{ij}, and is specified by a corresponding weighting coefficient, a_{ij}. Thus, the equation to reconstruct any EP_i is of the form:

$$EP_i = a_{i1}F_1 + a_{i2}F_2 + \ldots + a_{ik}F_k.$$

Although this result may surprise some readers, it might be made more intuitively obvious if presented in more familiar terms. Imagine that each member of a set of EPs had been subjected to Fourier analysis, describing the EP wave as a sum of oscillations at different frequencies, with a coefficient defining the amount of each frequency contributing to each EP waveshape. Now, if each EP in the set had a qualitatively unique shape, the coefficients of the different frequencies describing each wave would differ from EP to EP. If all the EPs had exactly the same shape, all the terms in the Fourier series would be identical. If the set contained a limited number of possible shapes, less than the number of EPs, then those EPs with similar shapes would share similar weighting coefficients on certain terms in the Fourier series; that is, there would be a high degree of covariance between the group of coefficients describing that part of the wave that was common to those EPs. The factor waveshapes yielded by the procedure described above are simply the inverse transforms of each group of Fourier coefficients with high covariance. They provide a more parsimonious way to describe sets of EPs than Fourier analysis, and reflect the fact that normal brains can produce only a limited variety of EP waveshapes from a particular location under well-specified conditions.

For each of the K factors that describe the set of n EPs, it is possible to construct the distributions of weighting coefficients, a_{ij}. The essential properties of the factor description of the EP signal space are:

1. the number of factors needed to reconstruct a large number of normal EPs is limited;
2. certain factors contribute more to some EP waveshapes than others;
3. the range of weighting coefficients contributed to a particular EP in a large normal population tends to be normally distributed for each factor.

The distributions of weighting coefficients a_{ij}, for each of the K factors describing a set of n EPs, define the variations in the contribution of the corresponding factor waveshape to that set of EPs. In the K-dimensional factor space, the resulting distributions of factor scores define a *hyperellipsoid;* that is, the volume containing the weighting coefficients likely to be required for any of the K factors in order to reconstruct any EP recorded from a particular lead in any normal person under specified conditions, to within a certain residual variance. The hyperellipsoid can be considered as a probability density defining the likelihood of the contribution of any particular factor to the reconstruction of any normal EP.

Mahalanobis Distance for an Individual EP

This set of analytical operations was carried out for a sample of EPs from a group of normal children, for every lead of the 10/20 system for every EP item in the NB for which a sufficiently large sample of data had been gathered. A total of 1,178 factor analyses were carried out for this purpose (19 leads times 62 items). In every instance, it proved possible to describe a large number of normal EPs with a much smaller number of factors, to better than 90 percent accuracy. In other words, no matter what lead or item, the apparent diversity of EP waveshapes could be explained as the sum of varying amounts of a small number of basic constituents, presumably corresponding to the action of different functional neuroanatomical systems. By this procedure, we defined the normal hyperellipsoid for every lead and EP item.

It was now possible to construct the linear combination of factors that best described the morphology of the EP obtained from any individual child at a particular lead during a specific EP item of the NB. The combination of weighting coefficients most probable for accurate reconstruction of any EP from a normal person is defined by the *center* of the hyperellipsoid of weighting coefficients, for any lead under any condition. The *distance* between the vector representing the individual EP and the center of the normal hyperellipsoid in the K-dimensional space corresponding to that lead and item could be computed, and was called the *Mahalanobis distance*. During our initial evaluations of this multivariate morphology metric, we had inadequate norms to estimate the significance of any absolute value of the Mahalanobis distance. For this reason, we developed a *relative* metric, which is called the *likelihood ratio*. This is the ratio of the probabilities that an individual EP lies outside versus inside the normal hyperellipsoid. High values of the likelihood ratio imply that the observed EP morphology would be extremely improbable in a sample of EPs from normal children.

Note that these multivariate descriptors take the intercorrelations between successive time points along the EP analysis epoch into consideration. For this reason, significant differences found with this metric are more statistically robust and meaningful than t-tests between group Grand Averages at individual time points, as discussed in chapter 7.

Distributions of Mahalanobis Distance Likelihood Ratios in N and LD Groups for Every 10/20 Lead and NB Item

Once the hyperellipsoid of the normal EP space had been defined for each electrode in the 10/20 system and every EP item in the NB, the Mahalanobis distance was calculated for the EP waveshapes obtained from each of the nineteen leads in each individual member of the sample of normal and of learning disabled children from whom data had been recorded on each NB item. Intelligence, achievement, and other psychometric tests had been administered to all of these children to confirm that all members of both groups were of normal intelligence, that all children included in the normal group were at grade level in verbal and arithmetic skills, and that all children included in the LD group actually were academic underachievers.

Each Mahalanobis distance value was then converted to a likelihood ratio, and the significance of differences in the distribution of likelihood ratios between the N and LD groups was evaluated using the t-test. Note that the samples of N and LD children used to construct the distributions of likelihood ratios consist of those used to construct the Grand Average EPs *minus* the randomly selected sets of normal children used to define the normal hyperellipsoid for each EP item. *In no instance was the likelihood ratio for EP data from a normal child included in these distributions if those data had been utilized in the process of defining the normal EP space.* Thus, the distributions of likelihood ratios evaluated in table 25 test the validity of the definition of the normal hyperellipsoid for each lead and item, using *independent* sets of normal children.

In this way, it was possible to evaluate the significance of differences in the incidence of EPs with unusual morphology, in *individual members* of N and LD groups. In chapter 7, we described the construction of Grand Average EPs and variances for groups of normal and LD children, computation of the N-LD difference waves, and t-tests for the significance of the differences between the N and LD groups *as a whole.*

For each 10/20 lead and every EP item in the NB, it was now possible to evaluate whether there were significant differences in the morphology of the EP between normal and learning disabled *individuals* as well as *groups.* If the features of Grand Average EPs and variances reflected appreciable homogeneity of morphology within the N and LD groups (for a given lead and item), then the results of examining EP waveshapes by individuals and by groups should be concordant. Whether the differences were found to be significant or not significant, the two methods should concur. However, if the features of Grand Average EPs and variances reflected appreciable heterogeneity causing high variance within either or both the N and LD groups, the N-LD difference wave might not reach significance, though subgroups whose members showed highly unusual EP morphology might cause significant differences between the N and LD groups in the distribution of likelihood ratios. Conversely, Grand Average EPs and N-LD difference waves might show significance for small but consistent differences in the amplitude of a component localized to a relatively short interval in the latency epoch. Such temporarily restricted differences would cause only minor alterations in the Mahalanobis distance of individual EPs and would probably not reach significance.

Table 25 contains twenty *columns* of data, one for each 10/20 lead plus one for the total Mahalanobis distance computed *across* all leads, and eighty-six *rows,* one for every EP condition and challenge of the full NB. Data for *both* the significances of the difference waves between Grand Average EPs from N and LD groups *and* of the distribution of likelihood ratios for the Mahalanobis distances of EPs from individual members comprising those groups were available for items 30–98.

For items 99–115, it proved all but impossible to obtain data from LD children, who almost invariably refused to submit to testing as soon as the conditioning procedure was described or shortly after testing on these items began. The size of the sample of LD data was therefore too small for meaningful N versus LD comparisons. However, data were obtained from enough normal children to provide interesting information about EP changes in conditioning.

If the *N-LD difference wave* between the Grand Average EPs for any 10/20 lead and NB item from the two groups was statistically significant at least at the $p \leq .01$ level, at any latency in the analysis epoch, the entry D was made at the corresponding position in table 25. If the distributions of *likelihood ratios for the Mahalanobis distances* of EPs for any 10/20 lead and NB item from members of the N and LD groups were significantly different at least at the $p \leq .01$ level, the entry M was made at the corresponding position in table 25. If *both* the N-LD difference wave and the distribution of the likelihood ratios were significantly different for any lead and item, the entry B was made. For items 99–115, only the Grand Average EPs and variances of the normal children were analyzed, with reference to the normative waveshapes. If the Grand Average waveshapes of the normal group during some item were significantly different from the reference at least at the $p \leq .01$ level, the entry was made at the corresponding position. Such findings simply indicate that the sensory-sensory conditioning procedure yielded those significant EP changes *within* the normal group.

Of the 1,380 lead-item "cells" for which N-LD differences were computed in table 25, 267 or 19.4 percent showed significant N-LD difference waves, 165 or 11.9 percent showed unusual EP morphology significantly more in members of the LD group than among the normals, and 60 or 4.4 percent showed significant intergroup differences by both measures. Thus, a total of 35.8 percent of the cells showed differences significant at the $p \leq .01$ level between the EP waveshapes of N versus LD children on pooled group measures, measures of the morphology of EPs from individual members of the two groups, or both. This is far beyond the incidence of differences reasonably attributable to chance. The precise number of significant N-LD differences expected by chance cannot be estimated, since the amount of independence of successive t-tests across the analysis epoch is not known. For the Mahalanobis distance, fourteen differences at the $p \leq .01$ level would be expected by chance. This establishes unequivocally that differences in the waveshapes of EPs recorded from normal and LD children are pervasive. They can be found at any electrode location, although they are somewhat more frequently encountered at C_3, T_3, P_3, P_z, O_1, P_4, C_4, and T_5, in that order. They seem somewhat higher in incidence on the left hemisphere than the right, and they seem to occur less frequently in frontopolar and frontal leads than elsewhere, which may simply reflect the lower signal to noise ratio and greater variability of EPs in those regions.

The high incidence of waveshape abnormalities, in conjunction with the significance of N-LD difference waves, indicates that for certain EP items, waveshape anomalies of a *similar sort* must exist within a substantial proportion of the LD sample. The number of leads showing anomalous waveshapes in a significantly greater proportion of LD than normal children for each EP item was slightly above 7.1 per item on the average, ranging from seventeen for focused video plus tap (item 89) to zero for the initial rate of rehabituation (item 53).

Every one of the different classes of EP items yielded significant intergroup differences in EP morphology. Appreciable variation in the incidence of significant differences was found within the set of items belonging to each class. For obscure reasons, items that seem reasonably comparable (for example, large square and small diamond, or the letters *b* and *p*) can differ markedly in the sharpness with which they reveal intergroup differences. We find it remarkable that almost every one of the sixty-nine EP items for which sufficient data were available revealed significant intergroup differences at several electrode sites. Although the sites showing the clearest effect varied from class to class of EP item, as expected, reasonable consistency was found within the several items belonging to the same class. Basic similarities were also found among the N-LD difference waves at a given lead for items belonging to the same class. This high interval consistency confirms the reliability of this large body of observations.

The various classes of EP items were ranked for sensitivity, according to the average number of leads showing significant differences across all the items within each class, as follows:

Habituation	10.7 (items 39–48)
Visual Figure-Ground Relations	9.8 (items 84–92)
Auditory Figure-Ground Relations	9.1 (items 93–98)
Perception of Geometric Forms	8.6 (items 67–74)
Perception of Letters	7.0 (items 75–83)
Sensory Acuity and Visual Contrast	5.8 (items 62–66)
Perception of Temporal Order	5.2 (items 30–38)
Rate of Habituation	3.3 (items 49–56)
Memory of Habituation	3.0 (items 57–61)

Sensory-Sensory Conditioning

Although insufficient data were obtained on the items belonging to the sensory-sensory conditioning class, because this paradigm was not well tolerated by most LD children in our sample, it was possible to evaluate quantitatively the changes produced in the EP elicited in normal children by the conditioned stimulus (CS) and unconditioned stimulus (US) as a result of both the pairing of flash (CS) followed by click (US) and the pairing of click (CS) followed by flash (US). Examination of the data for items 103–9 in table 25 shows the effects of the conditioning procedure. Significant changes in the EP to the flash CS after conditioning (item 103) were found in numerous regions, including C_3 and C_4 where they would be expected on the basis of previous reports. However, since comparable changes in the EP to the click US (item 104) and the neutral control tap stimulus (item 105) occurred in the same region, such changes can reasonably be attributed to sensitization and/or pseudoconditioning. In contrast, the changes in the EP to the click CS after conditioning (item 108) were much more marked than to the flash US (item 107) or the pseudoconditioning control (item 109), especially in O_1 and O_2 where they would be expected from prior studies. Although some signs of sensitivity or pseudoconditioning were formed, they were weaker and in large part were located in regions other than those that showed enhanced response to the click CS. Thus, our results indicate that far better sensory-sensory conditioning can be obtained with a click CS and flash US than vice versa. However, at least using the paradigm we selected, this procedure is so tedious as to be unusable for routine evaluation of learning disabled children.

Discrimination between N and LD Children Using
the Mahalanobis Distance of Individual EPs

In order to test the utility of the Mahalanobis distance to discriminate between normal and learning disabled children, we first studied the distribution of likelihood ratios for a normal and a learning disabled group.

The results presented above demonstrated significant and consistent differences between the distributions of likelihood ratios for the Mahalanobis distance in groups of N and LD children on many leads and EP items. Since we had not yet developed sufficient normative data to permit Z transformation of the Mahalanobis distance, it was necessary to learn more about the actual distribution of likelihood ratios in order to establish reasonable criteria for the use of these indices to classify individual EP waveshapes. Accordingly, for a representative sample of EP items that we selected, we examined the actual distribution of likelihood ratio values in the N and LD groups for the lead that showed the highest t-test.

On the average across these presumably typical distributions, 94.4 percent of the measures from normal children had a likelihood ratio between 0 and 2, and only 2 percent had a likelihood ratio above 3. Thus, a likelihood ratio of 2 was roughly equivalent to the $p = .05$ level, and a likelihood ratio of 3 to the $p = .01$ level. In contrast, 28.1 percent of the measures from the LD group showed a likelihood ratio greater than 2, and 14.1 percent had a likelihood ratio greater than 3. Accordingly, we decided to adopt a likelihood ratio of 2 as the maximum value for the Mahalanobis distance of an EP that we would consider within the limits of normal morphology, while EPs with a value greater than 2 would be classified as abnormal.

Using these criteria, we classified EPs from the N and LD groups for selected leads and items. Since classification of all the available data from every lead and item would have required a prohibitive amount of computation, we analyzed only data from those leads and items for which the most significant intergroup differences had previously been found for the distributions of likelihood ratios. For those few items on which no lead showed significant intergroup differences, data were analyzed from the lead with the highest value on the t-test. Each of these sets of EPs, of course, were classified with respect to the normal hyperellipsoid previously defined for the corresponding lead and item, and data from children used to define the normal EP space were always excluded from these computations. Inspection of these data reveals a wide range of classification accuracy. False positives vary from 0 percent to 30 percent, while correct classification of EPs from LD children varies from 0 percent to 63 percent. In many instances, a very low incidence of false positives is combined with a high incidence of correct classification of EPs from LD children. The significance of the difference between the N and LD distributions was assessed by chi-square. Inspection of table 26 shows that seven NB items yielded significant difference at levels between $p < .05$ and $.001$. Each entry in table 27 consists of two numbers: the first number is the percentage of EPs from normal children erroneously classified as false positives, and the second is the percentage of EPs from LD children correctly classified as abnormal.

We made no attempt to estimate the statistical significance of these classifications, because we felt that the marked differences in sample sizes for the different sets of data might easily lead to erroneous conclusions about the relative utility of data from particular leads or EP items for the identification of abnormal EP morphology. The leads and items selected for this table were those that showed the most significant differences for the distributions of likelihood ratios. However, examination of the data in table 27 supports several conclusions. The classification accuracy of data from certain leads and EP items seems quite robust and potentially useful, while the utility of data from other cells in the lead-by-item matrix seems quite dubious. One can obviously make trade-offs between few or no false positives, with moderate levels of correct identification of abnormal EPs, and larger numbers of false positives, with high levels of identification of abnormality. Overall, these findings unequivocally demonstrate that a very high proportion of the EPs obtained from LD children display abnormalities of morphology, whereas normal children show a much lower incidence of such abnormal EP waveshapes. The Mahalanobis distance of an individual EP from the center of a normal hyperellipsoid appears to provide an objective and quantitative metric for overall waveshape morphology, with potential diagnostic utility. Judicious selection of a relatively small set of 10/20 leads and EP items, together with appropriate multivariate analysis, might eventually permit the construction of EP test batteries that would be optimal for various diagnostic purposes, with minimum false positives and maximum identification of true abnormalities. The classification accuracy of any single univariate feature alone, not surprisingly in view of the heterogeneity of the LD population, was inadequate for this purpose.

CHAPTER 9

EP Feature Extractors

Normative Data

Encouraged by these results, we undertook to develop a set of methods to extract various quantitative features from the EP that we considered to be of probable diagnostic value, to gather sufficient normative data on these features to provide reliable age-regressed estimates of their mean values and standard deviations in healthy children, and to evaluate the distribution of Z-transformed values of these measures on a core set of NB EP items in additional groups of N and LD children.

The set of EP feature extractors was intended to provide objective indices of the amplitude, the signal-to-noise ratio, the waveshape symmetry, the amplitude asymmetry, the significance of the amplitude asymmetry, and the morphology of EPs from individual or homologous pairs of 10/20 leads. Details of these measures were presented in chapter 3. These measures were selected after a period of evaluating a much larger set of features on a pilot sample of EPs from small groups of N and LD children. Features that did not display or could not be normalized to give approximately Gaussian distributions in normal children, that had excessively large standard deviations, or that revealed little or no utility for differentiating between sets of EPs from N and LD children were discarded.

The measures selected for inclusion in the set of EP features to be more fully evaluated are listed below. It may be helpful to indicate the intent of each of these indices: *log mean power* provides an estimate of average size of the EP independent of polarity; *log maximum signal to noise* provides an estimate of the ambiguity of the signal; *log mean difference power* provides an estimate of the average amplitude asymmetry between homologous pairs independent of whether either side is always greater or which side is greater; *log maximum difference signal to noise* provides an estimate of the consistency or significance of an amplitude asymmetry; a *log function of the correlation coefficient* between homologous pairs was evaluated to obtain an estimate of the bilateral symmetry of wave shape; and finally, the *Mahalanobis distance* provides an estimate of the probability that the EP is of normal morphology.

Each of the above features was extracted from the EPs of 122 normal male and female children six to fourteen years old, of normal intelligence and performing at grade level in verbal and arithmetic skills both in school and on achievement tests (WRAT), for every lead of the 10/20 system, for the following items of the *core NB:* random 45 dB clicks (item 34), regular 45 dB clicks (item 31), blank flash (item 62), 7 lines-per-inch grid (item 63), 27 lines-per-inch grid (item 64), letter *b* (item 75), and letter *d* (item 76). Each of the six features was computed across four subepochs selected by examining the latency histograms presented in table 24: 50–120 ms, 120–290 ms, 300–500 ms, 0–500 ms. For each of these twenty-four features, every individual value was corrected for subject age by linear regression, and the mean value and standard deviation for each lead and item was calculated across the population of 122 normal children. These procedures yielded a set of normative data consisting of more than 2,600 means and standard deviations.

Further pilot studies were carried out on these features, studying Z-transformed values from a small group ($n = 25$) of N and LD children. As a result of these studies, we reached the following conclusions: (1) Data from the 50–120 ms and 120–290 ms analysis subepochs had little diagnostic utility because of the extremely high incidence of false positive findings. (2) The log function of the correlation coefficient had little diagnostic utility, both because it was insensitive both to amplitude asymmetries and to temporally localized waveshape asymmetries.

Although normative symmetry values were quite high by this measure, EPs from LD children seldom displayed significant deviations from these values. (3) For log maximum signal to noise and log maximum difference signal to noise, only *negative* Z values usefully discriminated between EPs from N and LD children. That is, for *signal-to-noise features, only significantly low values were of diagnostic utility.* (4) For log mean difference power, only *positive* Z values discriminated. That is, *LD children displayed significantly larger power asymmetries than normal.* (5) For log mean power, both *negative* and *positive* Z values discriminated. That is, *LD children displayed extreme values of EP power, unusually high as well as unusually low.* And (6) for Mahalanobis distance, we found that *using a 120–290 ms epoch minimized the incidence of false positives.* This confirmed the inference, drawn from table 24, that morphology differences would be most likely to occur in this latency domain. To define the normal hyperellipsoid for each set of 122 EPs, twelve factors were used, yielding an average EP reconstruction accuracy of 94 percent.

Sensitivity of EP Features to Brain Dysfunctions Related to Learning Disabilities

The pilot studies just described thus left us with a basic set of eleven EP features:

1. Log maximum signal to noise, negative Z values, 300–500 ms.
2. Log maximum signal to noise, negative Z values, 0–500 ms.
3. Log mean power, negative Z values, 300–500 ms.
4. Log mean power, positive Z values, 300–500 ms.
5. Log mean power, negative Z values, 0–500 ms.
6. Log mean power, positive Z values, 0–500 ms.
7. Log mean difference power, positive Z values, 300–500 ms.

8. Log mean difference power, positive Z values, 0–500 ms.
9. Log maximum differences signal to noise, negative Z values, 300–500 ms.
10. Log maximum differences signal to noise, negative Z values, 0–500 ms.
11. Mahalanobis distance from normal hyperellipsoid, 100–260 ms.

These features were then computed for each lead of the 10/20 system and for each EP item of the core NB for the four groups of children defined as follows: A new group of normals, *Group I* (N_1) consisted of 62 normal male and female children from six to fifteen years old, with IQs above 90, performing at grade level in school and on achievement tests (WRAT). *Group II* (LD) consisted of 56 male and female children from six to sixteen years old with IQs between 64 and 84 attending a special school for children unable to learn satisfactorily in their local schools (this group was identical with Group 7, whose EEG data were evaluated in chapter 4). In the data presented in this section, *Group III* (N_2) refers to another new group of 122 normal children who were used to construct the EP normative data base. *Group IV* (SLD) consisted of 49 male and female children from six to sixteen years old with IQs above 85, most of whom were attending their local schools but performing at least two grades below their appropriate level in language skills, arithmetic skills, or both, on the WRAT as well as in school (these children were the members of Group 6, whose EEG data were evaluated in chap. 4 and for whom data on the EP items of the core NB were also available).

Grand Average EPs were constructed for all four groups and are shown in figure 21, for all five visual EP items of the core NB, to permit visual comparison of waveshapes between Groups I (N_1) and III (N_2), and between Groups II (SLD) and IV (LD). Figure 22 illustrates the Grand Average difference waves, from lead O_1, for N_1 versus N_2, N_1 versus LD, N_1 versus SLD, LD

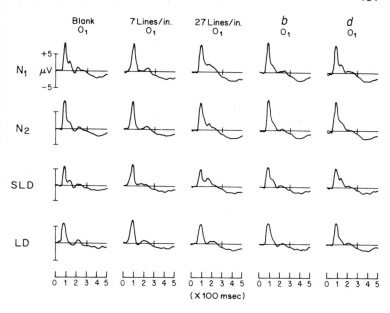

Fig. 21.   Grand Average EPs for different groups

versus N_2, LD versus SLD, and N_2 versus SLD for each EP item. Figure 23 presents the significance of these differences. The basic similarities between the Grand Averages from the two normal groups and between the SLD and LD groups are apparent by inspection of these figures.

Table 28 presents the number of values significant at the .01 and .001 levels for each of the basic eleven EP features, summed across all leads of the 10/20 system and across every EP item in the core NB, for each of the four groups of children. The features are identified in the key at the bottom of the table. Since the total number of measures computed for each feature on every EP item is 19 times n, where n is the size of the group, the chance number of Z values significant at the $p = .01$ level for the four groups are respectively twelve, nine, twenty-three, and eleven. For Group I, the chance level of false positives is

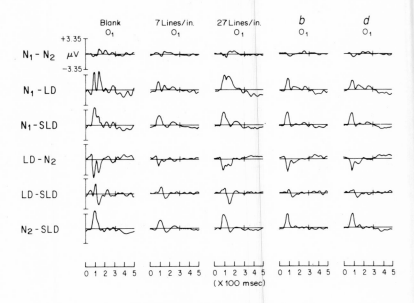

Fig. 22.   Intergroup difference waves

exceeded only by seven features, such as the Mahalanobis distance for regular click and blank flash. For Group III, the chance level is not even approached, for any feature. For Group II, the chance level is exceeded by thirty-four of seventy-seven feature distributions, and for Group IV by nineteen of seventy-seven feature distributions.

These data show that the distribution of Z values for these EP features on the EP items of the core NB lies within the expected limits for the normal children, with few exceptions, while a significant proportion of the EPs from LD children lie beyond the limits predicted by the distribution of the normative data. Certain analysis subepochs and EP items seem to yield fewer false positives and more correct identifications of abnormality than others. However, since one neither knows the redundancy of the set of feature extractors and EP items nor has access to the iden-

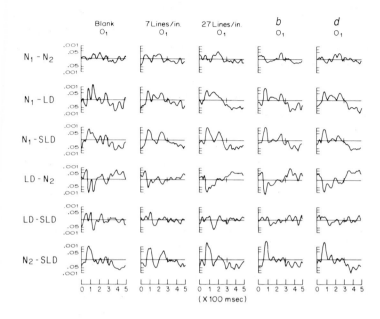

Fig. 23. Significance of differences for intergroup difference
waves

tity of the individuals classified as normal or abnormal by the
various features and items, examination of group distributions
alone are inadequate to evaluate the diagnostic utility of the full
data set. The distributions of Z values in table 28 simply demonstrate that the set of EP feature extractors are sensitive to the
brain dysfunctions in children with learning disability. The
significance of intergroup differences is tested in table 29.

Overall Utility of EEG and EP Features Extracted
from NB Items for Discrimination between N and
LD children

Given the large number of variables provided by the EEG and
EP features that we extracted from NB items, it is difficult to

reach a reliable estimate of the discrimination accuracy of the full body of available data. The various discriminant analyses that we have presented have been essentially uni- or pauci-variate and pragmatic, rather than analytical. In the long run, *a reliable estimate can only be obtained by construction of a stepwise multiple discriminant function that effectively separates a mixed group of normal and learning disabled children, and the subsequent replication of this classification accuracy in a double-blind study with accurate results.* Unfortunately, we have not been able to obtain the research funds necessary to accomplish this validation—a discriminant function using jack-knife replication has previously been published (John et al. 1983).

Most statisticians concur that in order to achieve a stepwise multiple discriminant function that accurately separates target populations and that can be independently replicated, one needs at least five times as many subjects and preferably ten times as the number of variables to be evaluated. Given the enormous number of variables provided by the full NB, with numerous features extracted from each lead for each item, it is imperative to prune the variable set down to a small number of especially promising features by strategies like those we have discussed.

Having reduced the full NB to the core NB, and having pruned our feature set down to a relatively small set compared to what we started with, we were now in a position to construct a first estimate of the relative utility of the features and of the overall diagnostic utility of the core NB for learning disabilities, using the distributions of the EEG and EP features discussed above. For the 40 EEG spectral estimators, we defined as abnormal any child who displayed more than 6 values above the .05 level. For the 32 EEG coherence and power asymmetry measures, we considered as abnormal any child who displayed more than 4 values above the .05 level, more than 2 values above the .01 level, or more than 1 value above the .001 level. For the 114 Mahalanobis distance values (19 leads times 6 EP items), we considered as abnormal any child who displayed more than 5 values above the .05 level, more than 2 values above the .01 level, or any single value above the .001 level. For the 1,330 EP feature values (19 leads times 7 EP items times 10 features per item), we considered as abnormal any child who displayed more than 7 values above the .01 level, or any single value above the .001 level.

Table 30 shows the distribution of hits on these various sets of EEG and EP features, alone and in combination, in groups of normal and learning disabled children. Total EEG hits in the two normal groups (I and III) were 8 percent and 12.3 percent respectively. In view of the quantitative nature of our analyses, this compares favorably with the 12 percent incidence of false positives found in ostensibly healthy individuals in conventional EEG examinations, evaluated by visual inspection of the records (Gibbs and Gibbs 1964). Groups II and IV showed a much higher incidence of abnormal EEG features, 45.9 percent and 44.6 percent respectively.

It is noteworthy that *none* of the children in Groups I and III who were false positives by EEG criteria were also false positives by EP criteria. In contrast, *about three-fourths of the children in Group II and two-fifths of those in Group IV who showed EEG hits also showed hits on EP features.* Spectral estimators and coherence features contributed equally to the EEG hits in the two LD groups, while coherence contributed somewhat more false positives than spectral estimators in the two normal groups. Group IV contained about twice as many children who only showed abnormal EEG features, as did Group II.

Group I showed about the same incidence of abnormal EP features as EEG, while Group III showed very few EP hits. Group II showed a very high incidence of EP hits, about one and one-half times that of EEG hits. One-half of the children in Group II who had EP abnormalities were normal by neurometric EEG criteria. Group IV showed about three-fourths as many EP as EEG hits. Again, one-half of the children in this LD group who had EP abnormalities were normal by neurometric EEG criteria. EP features other than the Mahalanobis distance constitute two-fifths of the EP hits in Group II, but most of the EP hits in Groups I and IV included abnormalities on this measure.

The overall accuracy of the set of criteria defined above seems quite good. The incidence of false positives in Groups I and III was closely comparable, being 19.4 percent and 15.5 percent respectively. *In view of the extremely large number of quantitative features here evaluated, for EPs as well as the EEG, this level of false positives seems acceptable, especially when compared with the 12 percent rate using conventional visual evaluation of the EEG alone. The NB is not intended as a mass screening technique but rather as a method for differential diagnosis. If we assume that only a small proportion of normal children will be considered sufficiently at risk to warrant this examination, the expected incidence of false positives does not seem prohibitive.*

The classification of LD children in Group II as abnormal was 77.1 percent, and of SLD children in Group IV, 62.5 percent. The relatively small discrepancy (15 percent) in detection of abnormality between these two groups may be due to the possibility that the SLD children, who are *differential* underachievers, seem more likely to be organically impaired with respect to *specific* aspects of brain function. The LD children, who cannot achieve sufficient academic competence to remain in their local schools, seem likely to include a substantial proportion of individuals with emotional or motivational problems as well as with diffuse brain dysfunctions.

In spite of the quantitative differences between Groups II and IV, the overall similarity of the findings in these two groups of children with learning problems, and the large disparity between the incidence of hits in these children versus the normal children in Groups I and III, can be considered to constitute a reasonably good replication of classification accuracy in two independent samples. These conclusions must be considered as tentative, pending an independent replication like that referred to above.

CHAPTER 10

Conclusions

We believe that we have constructed a quantitative and objective technique for evaluating features of the resting and evoked electrical activity of the brain, as a means for determining physiological bases for learning disabilities. Application of this technique to groups of normal and learning disabled children has demonstrated that false positives occur at or above the chance level in normal children, and true positives significantly above the chance level in learning disabled children. Abnormal features of brain electrical activity in LD children can be observed in any position of the 10/20 system and can be elicited by many different stimulus conditions. The anatomical loci at which abnormal features are found vary from child to child, and provide the basis for substantial functional heterogeneity within the learning disabled population. A distinction can be made between *developmental processes* or static functional interactions between anatomical regions (reflected in the features of the resting EEG), and *dynamic processes* related to the evaluation of information by the brain. Some LD children seem to suffer from maturational lag or imbalance between different neuroanatomical systems. In fact, using EEG measures, three types of LD children can be identified: (1) those for whom all deviations from predicted frequencies can be described as maturational lag; (2) those for whom all deviations can be described as developmental deviation; and (3) those for whom some brain regions can be described as maturational lag and others as developmental deviation (John et al. 1983). Other LD children seem to suffer primarily from more specific defects in information processing. In the latter group, attention should be directed toward the search for some brain mechanism that manifests itself with particular clarity in the interval between 200 and 260 milliseconds after the presentation of information relatively independent of the content of that information. Some aspects of our data suggest that the mesencephalic reticular formation may play a significant role in this mechanism.

The ultimate value of the method described in this monograph will lie in two directions: first, neurometric assessment should permit objective determination of whether learning disability in a particular individual should more plausibly be attributed to brain dysfunction or to other causes such as emotional, social, or motivational. Second, analysis of the anatomical locus of dysfunction and the nature of the dysfunctional processes may aid the development of analytical, individualized, prescriptive remediation, rather than the essentially undifferentiated methods that are currently used.

Appendixes

The Neurometric Battery

Set I. EEG Assessment of Structural Integrity and Maturation

Spontaneous and Resting EEG

Conditions

Item 1. Eyes-open, spontaneous EEG at the beginning of testing.
This condition yields eyes-open baseline EEG measures. A total of 60 seconds of computer artifacted EEG is recorded while the subject sits relaxed with eyes open, looking at a blank screen in a dimly lit testing room illuminated with a 15 watt red light. Ambient light in the room is .25 fc (foot candles). The test chamber was shielded so that light conditions remained constant. The screen was 5 feet from subject position.

Item 2. Eyes-closed, resting EEG at the beginning of testing.
This condition yields eyes-closed baseline EEG measures. Same procedure as above except the subject's eyes are closed.

Item 3. Eyes-open, spontaneous EEG at the end of testing.
This provides a short-term reliability test for eyes-open EEG data. A total of 60 seconds of computer artifact-free EEG is recorded after 1.5 to 2.0 hours of the evoked response testing session. The subject sits relaxed with eyes open as in item 1.

Item 4. Eyes-closed, resting EEG at the end of testing.
This provides a short-term reliability test for eyes-closed EEG data.

The reader is reminded that the subjects' task is passive in all conditions. They are told only to attend to stimuli, but they are not required to give any response. This paradigm was dictated because of our desire to develop a test battery that could be administered to subjects of any age and any level of verbal comprehension or ability to follow complex instructions or perform tasks requiring verbal or motor output. The significance of challenges between conditions is evaluated statistically.

Same procedure as above except the subject's eyes are closed. The child knows this is the last item in the test battery.

Challenges

Item 5.   Eyes-open minus eyes-closed EEG at the beginning of testing.
This reflects the effect of removal of visual input. The difference between items 1 and 2 is measured for every feature extracted from the EEG.

Item 6   Eyes-open minus eyes-closed EEG at the end of testing.
This is a replication of item 5, providing a short-term reliability estimate (item 3 minus item 4).

Item 7.   Eyes-open EEG, beginning, minus eyes-open EEG, end (item 1 minus item 3).
This gives an estimate of effects due to the state of the subject, such as anxiety about the test or fatigue due to testing, versus characteristic individual features displayed across states. This is a severe test of short-term reliability of the eyes-open measures, since state changes like those mentioned above can be expected.

Item 8.   Eyes-closed EEG, beginning, minus eyes-closed EEG, end (item 2 minus item 4).
This gives an estimate of short-term reliability of the eyes-closed EEG measures, as in item 7.

Set II. Photic Driving at 2.5, 5, 10, and 18 Hz

Conditions

This set of conditions measures the efficacy of photic driving of the EEG in the four broad spectral bands: delta, theta, alpha, and beta. Eyes-closed EEG recordings are obtained for 10 seconds during photic driving at four frequencies, one in the center of each of these bands. The frequencies are presented in the following order: 10, 2.5, 18, and 5 Hz. Two 2.5-second epochs of spontaneous EEG were also recorded, beginning 2.5 seconds and 7.5 seconds following the termination of photic driving at each frequency, to measure the persistent aftereffects of photic driving.

Stimulus Specifications

Driving light = 4 fc at *S* position, 50% modulation. (Background illumination is that of the dimly lit testing room, .25 fc.)

Item 9.   Photic driving of EEG in the delta band.
Ten seconds of EEG is recorded during presentation of sinusoidally modulated light at 2.5 Hz.

Item 10.   Spontaneous EEG 2.5 seconds after the end of delta photic driving.
2.5 seconds of EEG is recorded as a test of persistence of delta photic driving.

Item 11.   Spontaneous EEG 7.5 seconds after the end of delta photic driving.
2.5 seconds of EEG is recorded as a test of persistence of delta photic driving.

Item 12.   Photic driving of EEG in the theta band.
Ten seconds of EEG is recorded during presentation of sinusoidally modulated light at 5 Hz.

Item 13.   Spontaneous EEG 2.5 seconds after the end of theta photic driving.
2.5 seconds of EEG is recorded as a test of persistence of theta photic driving.

Item 14.   Spontaneous EEG 7.5 seconds after the end of theta photic driving.
2.5 seconds of EEG is recorded as a test of persistence of theta photic driving.

Item 15.   Photic driving of EEG in the alpha band.
Ten seconds of EEG is recorded during presentation of sinusoidally modulated light at 10 Hz.

Item 16.   Spontaneous EEG 2.5 seconds after the end of alpha photic driving.
2.5 seconds of EEG is recorded as a test of persistence of alpha photic driving.

Item 17.   Spontaneous EEG 7.5 seconds after the end of alpha photic driving.
2.5 seconds of EEG is recorded as a test of persistence of alpha photic driving.

Item 18.   Photic driving of EEG in the beta band.
Ten seconds of EEG is recorded during presentation of sinusoidally modulated light at 18 Hz.

Item 19.   Spontaneous EEG 2.5 seconds after the end of beta photic driving.

2.5 seconds of EEG is recorded as a test of persistence of beta photic driving.

Item 20.   Spontaneous EEG 7.5 seconds after the end of beta photic driving.
2.5 seconds of EEG is recorded as a test of persistence of beta photic driving.

Challenges

This set of challenges measures the reactivity and persistence of photic driving in each frequency band. Reactivity to visual input in a particular frequency band is computed for every EEG index by subtracting the measure obtained for the item 2 condition (eyes-closed, resting EEG) from the value of the comparable measure obtained during or after photic driving in each of the four frequency bands (items 9–20). This type of reactivity may be viewed as a way to estimate the *transfer function*. Results are expressed in absolute terms, i.e., change of energy in each band expressed in microvolts squared, and in relative terms, i.e., percent change of energy in each band.

Item 21.   Reactivity to visual input in the delta frequency band.
Photically driven EEG at delta frequency (item 9) minus eyes-closed, resting EEG (item 2).

Item 22.   Reactivity to visual input in the theta frequency band.
Photically driven EEG at theta frequency (item 12) minus eyes-closed, resting EEG (item 2).

Item 23.   Reactivity to visual input in the alpha frequency band.
Photically driven EEG at alpha frequency (item 15) minus eyes-closed, resting EEG (item 2).

Item 24.   Reactivity to visual input in the beta frequency band.
Photically driven EEG at beta frequency (item 18) minus eyes-closed, resting EEG (item 2).

Short-term and long-term persistence of photic driving can be evaluated similarly.

Set III. Habituation of EEG

Conditions

This set of conditions measures the effect of presentation of a sustained series of monotonous and inconsequential events that are reflected in the EEG rhythms; these data are later used for the "rate of habituation" challenge. Eyes-closed EEG is recorded while two minutes of stimulation with sinusoidal flicker at 10 Hz are presented. Results are evaluated analogous to set III.

Stimulus Specifications

Driving light = 4 fc at *S* position, 50% modulation. (Background illumination in dimly lit room, .25 fc.)

Item 25. *EEG habituation to 10 Hz sinusoidal flicker during the first 30 seconds.*

Item 26. *EEG habituation to 10 Hz sinusoidal flicker during the second 30 seconds.*

Item 27. *EEG habituation to 10 Hz sinusoidal flicker during the third 30 seconds.*

Item 28. *EEG habituation to 10 Hz sinusoidal flicker during the last 30 seconds.*

Challenges

The rate of habituation to sinusoidal driving at 10 Hz can be considered as an index of a rudimentary adaptive process, the inhibition of response to meaningless, slightly noxious afferent input. Such diminution of the effectiveness of meaningless stimulation is estimated by subtracting measurements of the EEG during the last period of habituation from the comparable EEG measures during the initial habituation period. Such changes are expressed in absolute and relative terms for each EEG index.

Item 29. *First 30 seconds of EEG habituation (item 25) minus last 30 seconds of EEG habituation (item 28) to sinusoidal driving at 10 Hz.*

The amount of habituation in the second and third periods can be similarly estimated.

Average Evoked Response Assessment of the Integrity of Sensory, Perceptual, Attention, and Cognitive Factors in Information Processing

Set IV. Predicting Temporal Order

Conditions

The regular and random presentations of visual, auditory, and somatosensory stimuli serve as the basis for the later challenges devised to assess prediction of temporal order. For the regular stimulus condition, a *regular sequence* of flash, click, and tap is presented at 1-second intervals. For the random stimulus condition, a *random sequence* of flash, click, and tap (counterbalanced or ordered) at 1-second intervals is administered (between the habituation and rehabituation conditions of Set V, which follows).

Stimulus Specifications

Flash. *5 microseconds duration, 2,000 beam candlepower per second (BCPS), produced by rear projection of a 50% transmission grid with 65 lines per inch onto a 30-by-30-inch milk glass screen placed 5 feet from the subject, subtending a visual angle of 7°.*

Click. *3 ms duration, 45 dB above ambient sound level, produced by a rectangular voltage pulse delivered to a speaker 3 feet above the center of the screen.*

Tap. *3 ms duration, 1.5 ounce 0.125 inch push delivered by a solenoid to the pad of the right index finger.*

Item 30. *Flash in the* regular *flash, click, tap sequence.*
The sample size for this item was 63 N, 32 LD.

Item 31. *Click in the* regular *flash, click, tap sequence.*
63 N, 34 LD.

Item 32. *Tap in the* regular *flash, click, tap sequence.*
63 N, 33 LD.

Item 33. *Flash in the* random *flash, click, tap sequence.*
55 N, 25 LD.

Item 34. *Click in the* random *flash, click, tap sequence.*
55 N, 25 LD.

Item 35. *Tap in the* random *flash, click, tap sequence.*
54 N, 25 LD.

Challenges

Differences between EP waveshapes elicited by predictable and unpredictable stimuli reflect the diminution of response to predictable events and can be used to assess whether the subject is monitoring the environment in a manner that recognizes predictable sequences of events.

Item 36. *Random minus* regular *flash (item 33 minus item 30).*
44 N, 25 LD.

Item 37. *Random minus* regular *click (item 34 minus item 31).*
55 N, 25 LD.

Item 38. *Random minus* regular *tap (item 35 minus item 32).*
54 N, 25 LD.

Set V. Habituation-Rehabituation

Conditions

The habituation and rehabituation conditions serve as the basis for a variety of indices of the rate of phasic (short term) and tonic (long term) habituation as well as the amount of dishabituation and the memory of habituation. The visual flash, auditory click, and somato-sensory tap of Set IV are simultaneously presented as a compound stimulus, delivered at regular 1-second intervals. Five compound stimuli constituted a group. The *habituation* condition consisted of 25 such groups, with 4 seconds between groups, and occurred after the *regular sequence* of Set IV. The *random sequence* of Set IV was then presented, and caused *dishabituation*. The rehabituation condition was then presented, and was identical to the habituation condition.

Item 39. *Habituation 1.*
First 5 groups of compound stimulus (flash plus click plus tap) at 1-second regular intervals (total = 25 compound stimuli). 55 N, 22 LD.

Item 40. *Habituation 2.*
Second 5 groups of compound stimulus. 55 N, 22 LD.

Item 41. *Habituation 3.*
Third 5 groups of compound stimulus. 55 N, 22 LD.

Item 42. *Habituation 4.*
Fourth 5 groups of compound stimulus. 55 N, 22 LD.

Item 43. *Habituation 5.*
Fifth 5 groups of compound stimulus. 55 N, 22 LD.

Item 44. *Rehabituation 1.*
First 5 groups of compound stimulus after interruption by random stimulus sequence. 52 N, 18 LD.

Item 45. *Rehabituation 2.*
Second 5 groups of compound stimulus after interruption. 52 N, 18 LD.

Item 46. Rehabituation 3.
Third 5 groups of compound stimulus after interruption. 52 N, 18 LD.

Item 47. Rehabituation 4.
Fourth 5 groups of compound stimulus after interruption. 52 N, 18 LD.

Item 48. Rehabituation 5.
Fifth 5 groups of compound stimulus after interruption. 52 N, 18 LD.

Changes during Habituation and Rehabituation (Phasic Habituation)

Challenges

These items reveal the rate and amount of suppression of information input about a meaningless and monotonous event; such suppression reflects the refocus of attention and short-term memory and is considered *phasic habituation.*

Item 49. Habituation 1 minus habituation 2.
55 N, 22 LD.

Item 50. Habituation 1 minus habituation 3.
55 N, 22 LD.

Item 51. Habituation 1 minus habituation 4.
55 N, 22 LD.

Item 52. Habituation 1 minus habituation 5.
55 N, 22 LD.

Item 53. Rehabituation 1 minus rehabituation 2.
52 N, 18 LD.

Item 54. Rehabituation 1 minus rehabituation 3.
52 N, 18 LD.

Item 55. Rehabituation 1 minus rehabituation 4.
52 N, 18 LD.

Item 56. Rehabituation 1 minus rehabituation 5.
52 N, 18 LD.

Memory of Previous Habituation (Tonic Habituation)

Challenges

By comparing rehabituation with initial phasic habituation, these challenges reveal whether suppression of meaningless input is facilitated by memory of previous experience. Such suppression reflects *tonic habituation.*

Item 57.   Habituation 1 minus rehabituation 1.
52 N, 18 LD.

Item 58.   Habituation 2 minus rehabituation 2.
52 N, 18 LD.

Item 59.   Habituation 3 minus rehabituation 3.
52 N, 18 LD.

Item 60.   Habituation 4 minus rehabituation 4.
52 N, 18 LD.

Item 61.   Habituation 5 minus rehabituation 5.
52 N, 18 LD.

Set VI. Visual Acuity and Contrast

Conditions

All visual stimuli were slides that were presented at the rate of 1 per sec. in blocks of 50 trials and were rear projected from a distance of 39.37 inches onto a 30-by-30-inch milky glass screen placed 5 feet from the subject. All stimuli were projected with a slide projector (Model 1660, GAF Corporation), in which the bulb was replaced by an electronic photo flash tube. The duration of the stimulus presentation was 5 microseconds, and the output of the flash was 2,000 BCPS. The square stimulus displays subtended a visual angle of approximately 7° per slide.

Item 62.   Blank flash.
This stimulus consisted of a 50% transmission slide, with a checkerboard pattern of 65 checks per inch. This pattern is seen as a blank grey flash. 55 N, 38 LD.

Item 63.   7 checks-per-inch grid.
This stimulus was a 50% transmission slide of a checkerboard in which the individual check size subtended a visual angle of approxi-

mately 32° per side on the screen. This pattern is seen as a grid unless visual acuity is worse than 20/200. 54 N, 38 LD.

Item 64.   27 checks-per-inch grid.

This stimulus was a 50% transmission slide of a checkerboard in which the individual check size subtended a visual angle of approximately 8° per side on the screen. This pattern is seen as an array of dots if visual acuity is approximately 20/20. 52 N, 27 LD.

Challenges

These challenges assess effects of changes in visual contrast. The expected changes are usually in the 100–160 ms latency domain.

Item 65.   Blank minus 7 lines-per-inch grid.

A significant difference means the visual acuity of the subject is at least 20/200. 54 N, 38 LD.

Item 66.   Blank minus 27 lines-per-inch dots.

A significant difference means the visual acuity of the subject is at least 20/20. 52 N, 27 LD.

Set VII. Perception of Geometric Forms and Shape Invariance

Conditions

All stimuli used in this set were presented as slides using the method described for Set VI. Each condition contributes to an estimate of perception of differences in geometric forms as well as preservation of shape invariance independent of size, as assessed by challenges (items 71–74).

Item 67.   Large square (1 inch squared).

Each side of the large square subtended a visual angle of approximately 7° per side, centrally located on the screen. 48 N, 32 LD.

Item 68.   Small square (0.25 inch squared).

Each side of the small square subtended a visual angle of approximately 3.5° per side, centrally located on the screen. 47 N, 32 LD.

Item 69.   Large diamond (1 inch squared).

The large diamond stimulus was identical to the large square (item 67), but was rotated 45°. 47 N, 31 LD.

Item 70.   Small diamond (0.25 inch squared).

The small diamond stimulus was identical to the small square (item 68), but was rotated 45°. 47 N, 29 LD.

Challenges

These challenges assess the ability to perceive differences in geometric form and to preserve shape invariance in spite of change in size.

Item 71.   Large square minus small square.
Absence of a significant difference indicates the preservation of shape invariance independent of size. 47 N, 32 LD.

Item 72.   Large diamond minus small diamond.
Absence of a significant difference indicates the preservation of shape invariance independent of size. 47 N, 29 LD.

Item 73.   Large square minus large diamond.
A significant difference reflects the perception of differences in geometric forms of equal size and contour. 47 N, 31 LD.

Item 74.   Small square minus small diamond.
A significant difference reflects the perception of differences in geometric forms of equal size and contour. 47 N, 29 LD.

Set VIII. Letter Perception

Conditions

All stimuli used in the set were presented as slides, using the same procedures described for Set VI. Each condition contributes (in items 75–79) to estimates of the ability to perceive differences between shapes of letters that are most commonly reversed. Each letter subtended a visual angle of approximately 3.5° by 2°, centered on the screen.

Item 75.   b.
52 N, 32 LD.

Item 76.   d.
31 N, 26 LD.

Item 77.   p.
25 N, 25 LD.

Item 78.   q.
24 N, 25 LD.

Challenges

These challenges assess the ability to achieve discrimination between letter forms and are useful for assessing reversal and inversion reading problems.

Interpretation of the absence of significant differences between these conditions is contingent upon the results obtained in Sets VI and VII.

Item 79. b minus d.
Absence of significant differences, especially in parietal areas, reflects difficulty in discriminating between these mirror images. 31 N, 26 LD.

Item 80. p minus q.
Absence of significant differences reflects difficulty in discriminating between these mirror images. 24 N, 25 LD.

Item 81. b minus p.
Absence of significant differences reflects difficulty in discriminating between these inverted images. 25 N, 25 LD.

Item 82. d minus q.
Absence of significant differences reflects difficulty in discriminating between these inverted images. 24 N, 25 LD.

Item 83. b minus q.
Absence of significant differences reflects difficulty in discriminating between these inverted mirror images. 24 N, 25 LD.

Set IX. Figure Ground Relations—Visual Figure

Conditions

A meaningful stimulus, consisting of a silent, color, popular television cartoon program, constituted a "visual figure" presented against a background of regular alternation of flash, click, and tap at 1-second intervals.

Stimulus Specifications

Visual, auditory, and tactile stimuli were the same as in previous conditions. The luminance of the defocused video was equated to the intensity of the light on the screen—and was seen as "snow." Focused video was of the same luminance, but meaningful patterns could be discerned.

Item 84.   Defocused video screen plush flash.
This condition serves as baseline control for item 90. 32 N, 26 LD.

Item 85.   Defocused video screen plus click.
This condition serves as baseline control for item 91. 32 N, 36 LD.

Item 86. Defocused video screen plus tap.
This condition serves as baseline control for item 92. 32 N, 26 LD.

In the following three test items, the focused video served as "visual figure," because meaningful information was presented.

Item 87. Focused video plus flash.
53 N, 29 LD.

Item 88. Focused video plus click.
52 N, 29 LD.

Item 89. Focused video plus tap.
53 N, 29 LD.

Challenges

These challenges reflect the dynamic structuring of figure-ground relationships that require discrimination between relevant "visual figure" and irrelevant "group," which was either ipsi-modal (video-visual) or cross-modal (video-auditory or video-somatosensory).

Item 90. Focused-video-plus-flash minus defocused-video-plus-flash.
This challenge reflects the effects of ipsi-modal (visual-visual) figure-ground interaction. 32 N, 26 LD.

Item 91. Focused-video-plus-click minus defocused-video-plus-click.
This challenge reflects the effects of cross-modal (visual-auditory) figure-ground interaction. 32 N, 26 LD.

Item 92. Focused-video-plus-tap minus defocused-video-plus-tap.
This challenge reflects the effects of a different cross-modal (visual-somatosensory) figure-ground interaction. 32 N, 26 LD.

Figure-Ground Relations—Auditory

Conditions

A meaningful auditory stimulus, consisting of a tape recording of a musical selection, constituted an "auditory figure" presented against a background of regular alternation of flash, click, and tap at 1-second intervals. The intensity of music was 45 dB SPL above noise level. A popular music selection was used.

Stimulus Specifications

Visual, auditory, and tactile stimuli were the same as in previous conditions.

Item 93.   Music plus flash.
50 N, 22 LD.

Item 94.   Music plus click.
50 N, 22 LD.

Item 95.   Music plus tap.
50 N, 22 LD.

In test items 93–95, the music served as "auditory figure," because meaningful information was presented.

Challenges

These challenges reflect the dynamic structuring of figure-ground relationships requiring discrimination between relevant "auditory figure" and irrelevant "ground," which was either ipsi-modal (music plus click) or cross-modal (music plus flash or music plus somatosensory).

Item 96.   Music-plus-flash minus flash.
Significant differences between these test items reflect the effects of cross-modal (auditory-visual) figure-ground interaction. 50 N, 22 LD.

Item 97.   Music-plus-click minus click.
This challenge reflects the effects of ipsi-modal (auditory-auditory) figure-ground interaction. 50 N, 22 LD.

Item 98.   Music-plus-tap minus tap.
This challenge reflects the effects of cross-modal (auditory-somatosensory) figure-ground interaction. 50 N, 22 LD.

Set X. Conditioned Response Evaluation

This set of items provides baseline data for unpaired stimuli before sensory-sensory conditioning, visual-auditory pairing, and unpaired postconditioning to assess the effects of conditioning and sensitization. It also serves as baselines for auditory-visual conditioning, auditory-visual pairing, and unpaired postconditioning to assess the effects of conditioning and sensitization after the second conditioning paradigm. The challenges quantify the assessments.

Conditions

The first three items reveal increases or decreases in the response of the brain to the sequential presentations of simple stimuli in different sensory modalities, to provide baseline control measures.

Item 99. Regular flash.
Stimulus specifications are the same as in the earlier flash-click-tap sequences.

Item 100. Regular click.
Stimulus specifications are the same as in the earlier flash-click-tap sequences.

Item 101. Regular tap.
Stimulus specifications are the same as in the earlier flash-click-tap sequences.

Item 102. Flash followed by click after 250 ms.
Item 102 carries out sensory-sensory conditioning using a visual conditioned stimulus (flash) and an auditory unconditioned stimulus (click). Two hundred paired stimuli are delivered at a rate of 1 per second.

Item 103. Regular flash.
This item provides a basis for assessing the presence of a conditioned response to the CS. (See item 110.)

Item 104. Regular click.
This item is the basis for assessing the occurrence of *sensitization,* that is, a change in response to the US. (See item 111.)

Item 105. Regular tap.
This item is the basis for assessing the occurrence of pseudoconditioning, that is, a generalized increase in response to unpaired stimuli. (See item 112.)

Item 106. Click followed by flash after 250 ms.
This item carries out sensory-sensory conditioning with the sensory modalities reversed; that is, using an auditory conditioned stimulus (click) and a visual unconditioned stimulus (flash).

Item 107. Regular click.
This item is the basis for estimating the presence of a specific conditioning effect to the CS. (See item 113.)

Item 108. Regular flash.
This item is the basis for assessing sensitization to the US. (See item 114.)

Item 109. Regular tap.
This item is the basis for assessing the occurrence of pseudoconditioning to an unpaired stimulus. (See item 115.)

Challenges

Assessment of specific conditioning effects is achieved using a visual conditioned stimulus and an auditory unconditioned stimulus.

Item 110.   Postconditioning flash (item 103) minus control flash (item 99).

Significant differences between these EPs reflect the effects of conditioning as specific changes in the response to the conditioned stimulus (flash).

Item 111.   Postconditioning click (item 104) minus control click (item 100).

This item provides a control for sensitization, which is revealed as a change to the unconditioned (click) as well as to the conditioned stimulus (flash).

Item 112.   Postconditioning tap (item 105) minus control tap (item 101).

This item provides a control for pseudoconditioning, which is revealed as a generalized change to any stimulus. Assessment of specific conditioning effects is achieved using an auditory conditioned stimulus and a visual conditioned stimulus.

Item 113.   Postconditioning click (item 107) minus control click (item 100).

Significant differences between these EPs reflect the effects of conditioning as specific changes in the response to the CS (click).

Item 114.   Postconditioning flash (item 108) minus control flash (item 99).

This item provides a control for sensitization, revealed as a change to the US as well as to the CS.

Item 115.   Postconditioning tap (item 108) minus control tap (item 101).

This item provides a control for pseudoconditioning, which is revealed as a generalized change to any stimulus.

APPENDIX 2

Tables

TABLE 1. Mean Psychometric Scores from N, LD, and SLD Groups

	PPVT	WISC V	WISC P	WISC F	WRAT R	WRAT S	WRAT A
N	118.95	—	—	—	120.79	116.10	108.13
N underachievers	108.80	—	—	—	105.75	97.81	87.63
SLD	100.24	93.03	98.54	95.34	88.35	84.41	81.39
SLD overachievers	101.57	88.14	92.14	92.40	101.53	102.59	97.29
LD	80.60	72.84	79.49	73.76	78.35	75.01	72.89

V = Verbal scale
P = Performance scale
F = Full scale
R = Reading
S = Spelling
A = Arithmetic

TABLE 2. Correlation Coefficients between Spectral Estimators from Edited and Unedited EEG

		N (A)	LD (B)	N (C)	LD (D)	N (E)
		$(n = 10)$	$(n = 10)$	$(n = 20)$	$(n = 20)$	$(n = 20)$
Δ	C_3C_z	.961	.980	.943	.969	.927
	C_4C_z	.976	.991	.866	.938	.922
	T_3T_5	.980	.959	.871	.919	.883
	T_4T_6	.981	.974	.879	.868	.920
	P_3O_1	.989	.955	.915	*	.925
	P_4O_2	.996	.960	.944	*	.943
	F_7T_3	.881	.931	.856	*	.869
	F_8T_4	.888	.903	.846	*	.839
Θ	C_3C_z	.988	.998	.939	.963	.877
	C_4C_z	.990	.999	.951	.963	.969
	T_3T_5	.998	.989	.967	.981	.978
	T_4T_6	.997	.988	.971	.886	.972
	P_3O_1	.986	.987	.982	*	.932
	P_4O_2	.987	.988	.971	*	.985
	F_7T_3	.969	.945	.908	*	.826
	F_8T_4	.977	.950	.895	*	.864
α	C_3C_z	.990	.992	.966	.952	.968
	C_4C_z	.995	.953	.972	.925	.983
	T_3T_5	.999	.994	.980	.974	.890
	T_4T_6	.994	.993	.980	.989	.983
	P_3O_1	.998	.984	.974	.985	.987
	P_4O_2	.996	.981	.981	*	.979
	F_7T_3	.990	.985	.980	*	.969
	F_8T_4	.996	.985	.965	*	.944
β	C_3C_z	.998	.998	.985	.969	.982
	C_4C_z	.998	.997	.981	.982	.985
	T_3T_5	.999	.985	.966	*	.928
	T_4T_6	.996	.928	.987	*	.993
	P_3O_1	.999	.994	.985	*	.995
	P_4O_2	.999	.970	.987	*	.996
	F_7T_3	.982	.984	.977	*	.970
	F_8T_4	.988	.930	.977	.929	.974
Average length of sample	Unedited	59.77	54.24	22.04	22.04	22.04
	Edited	42.36	39.70	24.02	24.40	24.02

*Correlations not computed

TABLE 3. Correlation Coefficients (n) between Coherence and Power Asymmetry Measures from Unedited and Edited Samples of EEG Data.

		N ($n = 10$)	LD ($n = 10$)
Coherence			
Δ	C	.977	.965
	T	.786	.922
	PO	.765	.911
	FT	.874	.753
θ	C	.982	.985
	T	.929	.976
	PO	.957	.958
	FT	.982	.840
α	C	.903	.995
	T	.998	.981
	PO	.975	.980
	FT	.989	.988
β	C	.912	.963
	T	.983	.962
	PO	.976	.914
	FT	.822	.881
Power Asymmetry			
Δ	C	.635	.927
	T	.924	.927
	PO	.928	.948
	FT	.393	.943
θ	C	.910	.978
	T	.982	.994
	PO	.983	.991
	FT	.915	.940
α	C	.962	.989
	T	.977	.988
	PO	.937	.992
	FT	.902	.934
β	C	.959	.991
	T	.996	.923
	PO	.944	.976
	FT	.969	.890

TABLE 4. Test-Retest Reliability, Correlation Coefficients between Data from Beginning and End of Session, Relative Power, Eyes-Closed EEG, $n = 23$

		Frequency Band				Average Across Bands
		Δ_2	Θ	α	β	
F_3	r	0.740	0.811	0.904	0.842	.824
	Z	4.255	5.057	6.687	5.485	
F_4	r	0.845	0.713	0.908	0.894	.840
	Z	5.545	3.995	6.779	6.438	
C_3	r	0.769	0.885	0.867	0.777	.825
	Z	4.547	6.249	5.916	4.645	
C_4	r	0.693	0.817	0.827	0.689	.757
	Z	3.810	5.137	5.269	3.783	
P_3	r	0.787	0.865	0.907	0.893	.863
	Z	4.753	5.876	6.748	6.423	
P_4	r	0.847	0.771	0.854	0.823	.824
	Z	5.567	4.577	5.686	5.211	
O_1	r	0.801	0.779	0.853	0.863	.824
	Z	4.931	4.663	5.663	5.839	
O_2	r	0.861	0.871	0.918	0.791	.860
	Z	5.793	5.979	7.037	4.806	
Average across leads	r	0.793	0.814	0.880	0.822	
Overall average reliability						.827

TABLE 5. Test-Retest Correlations over Varying Intertest Intervals (ITI) for Independent Learning Disabled Samples, Left-Hemisphere Derivations

ITI Sample		Age Corrected % Probability of Deviation (one-tailed)				Relative Power			
		LC	LT	LPO	LFT	LC	LT	LPO	LFT
0.00 years,	Δ	.60	.83	.76	.85	.86	.92	.78	.79
$n = 15$,	Θ	.63	.88	.95	.73	.79	.89	.91	.52
age = 11.67	α	.94	.94	.86	.96	.86	.97	.88	.80
	β	.56	.86	.48	.88	.86	.86	.62	.90
	$\Delta + \Theta$	.76	.80	.86	.88	.86	.85	.88	.79
0.62 years,	Δ	.79	.80	.76	.54	.81	.82	.74	.52
$n = 30$,	Θ	.74	.74	.94	.44	.84	.58	.75	.51
age = 10.06	α	.93	.79	.88	.61	.92	.88	.71	.87
	β	.86	.69	.49	.51	.87	.45	.47	.42
	$\Delta + \Theta$	.93	.78	.71	.57	.93	.73	.80	.46
2.46 years,	Δ	.40	.55	.49	.60	.42	.74	.57	.63
$n = 30$,	Θ	.83	.55	.60	.54	.90	.66	.79	.57
age = 9.40	α	.88	.87	.84	.56	.77	.77	.81	.67
	β	.82	.53	.46	.46	.75	.61	.63	.54
	$\Delta + \Theta$	.85	.63	.71	.57	.80	.67	.76	.65

TABLE 6. Values of the Coefficients for 16 Polynomial Functions % Power = $C_0 + C_1t + C_2t^2 + C_3t^3 + C_4t^4$

		C_0	C_1	C_2	C_3	C_4
F_7T_3/F_8T_4	Δ	52.88129044	-1.62412035	0.14557505	-.01315721	.00038862
	θ	24.06952286	1.48779488	-0.18975608	.00271877	.00008011
	α	6.26392508	1.47345734	-0.01208464	-.00123811	.00004093
	β	16.78528595	-1.33714950	0.05627370	.01167599	-.00051030
C_2C_3/C_2C_4	Δ	50.89767838	-6.48332644	0.73098153	-.04015033	.00077661
	θ	28.62268257	3.59762359	-0.61020833	.03214995	-.00060320
	α	10.37323475	4.44773149	-0.37918672	.01818673	-.00032878
	β	10.10641956	-1.56203568	0.25841025	-.01018707	.00015724
T_3T_5/T_4T_6	Δ	50.60667419	-5.91133118	0.71057779	-.04314391	.00089184
	θ	27.73017693	5.54276085	-1.20817029	.07555612	-.00156530
	α	4.90816212	3.00672746	0.26102471	-.03193251	.00090440
	β	16.75499535	-2.63816142	0.23657100	-.00048033	-.00023174
P_3O_1/P_4O_2	Δ	58.26884079	-11.62586880	1.46008492	-.08558909	.00178591
	θ	28.05751991	6.44061708	-1.55570507	.10411771	-.00224908
	α	5.54039478	6.15815401	-0.03854712	-.01701101	.00057141
	β	8.13325310	-0.97290999	0.13417210	-.0151845	-.00010862

TABLE 7. Values of Table 6 Converted to Log Units

		C_0	C_1	C_2	C_3	C_4
F_7T_3/F_8T_4	Δ	0.05026793	-0.02864339	0.00268197	-0.00024649	0.00000726
	θ	-0.49661124	0.02704753	-0.00219526	-0.00012897	0.00000637
	α	-1.19101954	0.11536730	-0.01021430	0.00052462	-0.00001035
	β	-0.69595569	-0.05826711	0.00636409	-0.00002820	-0.00000592
C_2C_3/C_2C_4	Δ	0.01337487	-0.11086171	0.01164788	-0.00062616	0.00001153
	θ	-0.39715552	0.07269696	-0.01230534	0.00065100	-0.00001268
	α	-0.94571376	0.17154604	-0.01993426	0.00110665	-0.00002212
	β	-0.95783710	-0.09368554	0.01825462	-0.00099472	0.00001902
T_3T_5/T_4T_6	Δ	0.01312087	-0.10731703	0.01305750	-0.00081664	0.00001665
	θ	-0.41266653	0.10212188	-0.02114789	0.00119691	-0.00002312
	α	-1.22848630	0.18772255	-0.01056178	0.00017109	0.00000299
	β	-0.70206171	-0.10165458	0.01017377	-0.00014639	-0.00000520
P_3O_1/P_4O_2	Δ	0.14496185	-0.20564358	0.02497562	-0.00150341	0.00003163
	θ	-0.41780865	0.13641311	-0.03206439	0.00204809	-0.00004317
	α	-1.14453661	0.25399819	-0.02050309	0.00080608	-0.00001157
	β	-1.06820560	-0.06939101	0.01273942	-0.00057574	0.00000711

163

TABLE 8. Standard Deviations of Log Relative Power for Each Frequency Band in Every Derivation

	Central	Temporal	Parieto-Occipital	Fronto-temporal
Δ	.17550	.19515	.22553	.13585
Θ	.19706	.21789	.21229	.13763
α	.27472	.25411	.26090	.18157
β	.14968	.20643	.17554	.19110

TABLE 9. Evaluation of Polynomial Functions Describing Relative Power in EEG Frequency Bands as a Function of Age and Derivation, Nine-Year-Old Male Children

		Swedish Children (n = 25)			New York City Children (n = 44)			
		Absolute Energy μV	Relative Power (%)	Polynomial Function	Mean Values of Relative Power			
					L	SD	R	SD
FT	Δ	14.2	44.9	44.1	39.6	8.7	39.7	9.3
	Θ	11.2	27.9	25.6	31.1	7.3	31.4	6.7
	α	9.1	18.4	16.8	16.2	6.8	18.0	7.0
	β	6.3	8.8	13.6	11.5	7.2	10.3	6.3
C	Δ	13.6	30.2	28.4	29.0	6.5	29.3	6.9
	Θ	14.8	35.8	32.3	35.8	8.4	37.0	8.1
	α	13.0	27.6	29.7	28.5	10.4	27.1	9.3
	β	6.2	6.3	9.6	5.6	2.2	5.6	2.5
T	Δ	15.5	27.9	30.4	29.3	7.8	29.8	8.3
	Θ	15.2	26.8	27.0	25.3	8.5	25.1	8.8
	α	17.9	37.3	33.0	34.8	15.1	35.6	15.3
	β	8.3	7.9	9.6	8.1	6.2	7.3	5.4
PO	Δ	16.8	21.7	22.2	24.6	9.3	25.4	8.2
	Θ	18.0	24.9	24.1	25.7	9.0	25.2	8.4
	α	24.8	47.3	46.1	43.0	15.1	42.3	14.5
	β	8.9	6.1	7.7	5.3	2.0	5.4	3.2

TABLE 10. Mean and Standard Deviation Values for Coherence and Power Asymmetry

		Coherence		200 [(L − R)/(L + R)] Power Asymmetry	
		Mean	SD	Mean	SD
F_7T_3/F_8T_4	Δ_2	34.5	20.0	−13.0	29.1
	Θ	20.8	14.8	−14.2	34.6
	α	21.4	10.6	−23.3	36.8
	β_1	19.8	14.0	−4.2	41.7
T_3T_5/T_4T_6	Δ_2	46.0	8.8	−7.4	35.0
	Θ	41.6	9.4	−5.0	33.0
	α	44.4	20.4	−8.1	45.7
	β_1	17.0	8.7	−1.0	46.5
C_3C_z/C_4C_z	Δ_2	36.1	14.7	2.2	32.1
	Θ	35.5	14.7	−0.9	25.3
	α	20.3	14.2	6.3	30.8
	β_1	16.4	13.0	4.7	23.7
P_3O_1/P_4O_2	Δ_2	55.8	9.8	−13.2	37.4
	Θ	57.4	8.7	8.0	33.3
	α	65.1	15.6	−8.2	37.9
	β_1	45.0	9.6	5.1	36.5

Note: These values are based upon analysis of the same samples of eyes-closed EEG from 44 healthy children used to compute the data in table 9. Note that no age regression function has yet been computed for these data.

TABLE 11. Distribution of Z Values for Spectral Power Estimators in Four Groups of Normal Children

		Group 1 ($n = 25$)				Group 2 ($n = 22$)			
		NS	.05	.01	.001	NS	.05	.01	.001
FT ($F_7T_3 + F_8T_4$)	$\Delta + \Theta$	45	5	0	0	44	0	0	0
	Δ	48	2	0	0	44	0	0	0
	Θ	47	3	0	0	42	2	0	0
	α	49	1	0	0	44	0	0	0
	β	44	6	0	0	44	0	0	0
T($T_3T_5 + T_4T_6$)	$\Delta + \Theta$	48	2	0	0	44	0	0	0
	Δ	49	1	0	0	44	0	0	0
	Θ	46	4	0	0	44	0	0	0
	α	47	3	0	0	44	0	0	0
	β	47	2	1	0	43	1	0	0
C($C_3C_z + C_4C_z$)	$\Delta + \Theta$	48	2	0	0	44	0	0	0
	Δ	50	0	0	0	43	1	0	0
	Θ	48	2	0	0	43	1	0	0
	α	50	0	0	0	44	0	0	0
	β	47	2	1	0	43	1	0	0
PO($P_3O_1 + P_4O_2$)	$\Delta + \Theta$	46	4	0	0	44	0	0	0
	Δ	49	1	0	0	44	0	0	0
	Θ	47	3	0	0	44	0	0	0
	α	44	3	3	0	44	0	0	0
	β	46	2	2	0	41	3	0	0
Total		945	48	7	0	871	9	0	0
%		94.5	4.8	0.7	0.0	99	1	0.8	0.3

		Spectral Power Estimators				Coherence + Power Asymmetry			
	n	NS	.05	.01	.001	n	NS	.05	.01	.001
Grand Total	5,600	5,429	132	38	1	4,480	4,202	185	77	16
%		96.95	2.36	0.68	0.02		93.80	4.13	1.7	0.36

Note: Chi-square and *p* are not significant.

NS = The number of cases with no significant departures from normality.

.05 = The number of cases with no significant departures from normal significance at the $p \le .05$ level.

.01 = The number of cases with no significant departures from normal significance at the $p \le .01$ level.

.001 = The number of cases with no significant departures from normal significance at the $p \le .001$ level.

	Group 3 (n = 52)				Group 4 (n = 52)		
NS	.05	.01	.001	NS	.05	.01	.001
103	1	0	0	80	2	0	0
103	1	0	0	80	0	1	1
102	2	0	0	79	2	1	0
101	3	0	0	80	2	0	0
88	8	8	0	76	3	3	0
104	0	0	0	82	0	0	0
104	0	0	0	82	0	0	0
102	2	0	0	81	1	0	0
102	2	0	0	81	1	0	0
95	4	5	0	75	5	2	0
100	4	0	0	80	2	0	0
97	5	2	0	81	1	0	0
103	1	0	0	80	2	0	0
102	2	0	0	82	0	0	0
97	5	2	0	78	3	1	0
104	0	0	0	81	1	0	0
102	2	0	0	82	0	0	0
102	0	2	0	82	0	0	0
102	0	2	0	81	1	0	0
98	4	2	0	79	3	0	0
2,011	46	23	0	1,602	29	8	1
96.7	2.2	1.1	0.0	97.7	1.8	0.5	0.1

	All EEG Neurometric Indices			
n	NS	.05	.01	.001
10,080	9,631	317	115	17
	95.54	3.14	0.14	0.17

TABLE 12.   Distribution of Z Values for Coherence and Power Asymmetry in Four Groups of Normal Children

		Group 1 ($n = 25$)				Group 2 ($n = 22$)			
		NS	.05	.01	.001	NS	.05	.01	.001
Coherence									
FT($F_7T_3 \, \nu \, F_8T_4$)	Δ	24	0	1	0	20	1	0	1
	Θ	25	0	0	0	19	1	1	1
	α	23	1	1	0	22	0	0	0
	β	22	2	1	0	21	1	0	0
T($T_3T_5 \, \nu \, T_4T_6$)	Δ	25	0	0	0	20	1	1	0
	Θ	23	1	0	1	20	2	0	0
	α	24	1	0	0	21	0	1	0
	β	24	1	0	0	21	1	0	0
C($C_3C_z \, \nu \, C_4C_z$)	Δ	24	0	1	0	20	1	1	0
	Θ	24	1	0	0	19	3	0	0
	α	25	0	0	0	18	3	0	1
	β	23	1	0	1	22	0	0	0
PO($P_3O_1 \, \nu \, P_4O_2$)	Δ	21	4	0	0	22	0	0	0
	Θ	24	0	1	0	22	0	0	0
	α	23	2	0	0	20	2	0	0
	β	23	2	0	0	22	0	0	0
Power asymmetry									
FT($F_7T_3 \, \nu \, F_8T_4$)	Δ	24	1	0	0	21	1	0	0
$200\frac{L-R}{L+R}$	Θ	25	0	0	0	19	2	1	0
	α	23	1	1	0	21	1	0	0
	β	25	0	0	0	21	1	0	0
T($T_3T_5 \, \nu \, T_4T_6$)	Δ	25	0	0	0	21	1	0	0
	Θ	24	1	0	0	21	1	0	0
	α	25	0	0	0	20	1	1	0
	β	23	1	1	0	20	2	0	0
C($C_3C_z \, \nu \, C_4C_z$)	Δ	25	0	0	0	21	1	0	0
	Θ	25	0	0	0	20	1	1	0
	α	24	0	1	0	20	2	0	0
	β	25	0	0	0	21	0	1	0
PO ($P_3O_1 \, \nu \, P_4O_2$)	Δ	25	0	0	0	21	0	1	0
	Θ	24	1	0	0	20	1	1	0
	α	23	2	0	0	21	1	0	0
	β	23	1	1	0	22	0	0	0
Total		765	24	9	2	659	32	10	3
%		95.6	3	1.1	0.2	93.6	4.5	1.4	0.4

Note: Chi-square and *p* are not significant. See table 11 for NS, .05, .01, and .001.

Group 3 (n = 52)				Group 4 (n = 41)			
NS	.05	.01	.001	NS	.05	.01	.001
50	0	1	1	35	5	0	1
48	3	1	0	37	2	2	0
52	0	0	0	39	2	0	0
49	2	0	1	39	2	0	0
46	1	2	3	35	1	4	1
47	3	1	1	40	1	0	0
50	1	1	0	41	0	0	0
49	2	1	0	37	2	2	0
50	1	1	0	35	4	2	0
49	1	0	2	40	0	1	0
49	2	1	0	38	2	0	1
49	3	0	0	40	1	0	0
51	1	0	0	40	1	0	0
50	2	0	0	41	0	0	0
50	0	2	0	41	0	0	0
51	1	0	0	40	1	0	0
46	4	2	0	34	4	3	0
47	4	1	0	34	5	2	0
47	2	3	0	37	4	0	0
49	0	3	0	35	2	4	0
50	2	0	0	40	1	0	0
50	1	1	0	40	1	0	0
49	3	0	0	40	1	0	0
46	4	2	0	35	3	3	0
48	4	0	0	39	2	0	0
44	6	2	0	40	1	0	0
46	5	1	0	39	1	1	0
48	3	1	0	41	0	0	0
50	2	0	0	38	2	1	0
51	0	1	0	40	1	0	0
48	2	2	0	34	5	2	0
48	3	1	0	37	4	0	0
1,557	68	31	8	1,221	61	27	3
93.5	4.1	1.9	0.5	93.1	4.6	2.1	0.2

TABLE 13. Distribution of False Positives Extracted from Eyes-Closed EEG in 140 Normal Children

Group	Spectral Power Estimators	Coherence and Asymmetry	Total
		$.05 \geq p > .01$	
1 ($n = 25$)			
False positives	48	24	72
Total measures	1,000	800	1,800
2 ($n = 22$)			
False positives	9	32	41
Total measures	880	704	1,584
3 ($n = 52$)			
False positives	46	68	114
Total measures	2,080	1,664	3,744
4 ($n = 41$)			
False positives	29	61	90
Total measures	1,640	1,312	2,952
Grand Total ($n = 140$)			
False positives	132	185	317
Total measures	5,600	4,480	10,080

170

.01 ≥ p > .001			.001 ≥ p		
Spectral Power Estimators	Coherence and Asymmetry	Total	Spectral Power Estimators	Coherence and Asymmetry	Total
7 / 1,000	9 / 800	16 / 1,800	0 / 1,000	2 / 800	2 / 1,800
0 / 880	10 / 704	10 / 1,584	0 / 880	3 / 704	3 / 1,584
23 / 2,080	31 / 1,664	54 / 3,744	0 / 2,080	8 / 1,664	8 / 3,744
8 / 1,640	27 / 1,312	35 / 2,952	1 / 1,640	3 / 1,312	4 / 2,952
38 / 5,600	77 / 4,480	115 / 10,080	1 / 5,600	16 / 4,480	17 / 10,080

TABLE 14. Distribution of Z Values of Spectral Power Estimators for Male and Female Children

		Female			Male		
		NS	.05 to .01	.01 to .001	NS	.01 to .01	.01 to .001
C_3C_z	Δ	28	0	0	28	0	0
	Θ	28	0	0	28	0	0
	α	28	0	0	28	0	0
	β	27	1	0	27	1	0
	$\Delta + \Theta$	28	0	0	28	0	0
C_4C_z	Δ	28	0	0	28	0	0
	Θ	28	0	0	28	0	0
	α	28	0	0	28	0	0
	β	27	1	0	27	1	0
	$\Delta + \Theta$	28	0	0	28	0	0
T_3T_5	Δ	27	1	0	27	1	0
	Θ	28	0	0	28	0	0
	α	26	2	0	25	3	0
	β	24	4	0	19	5	4
	$\Delta + \Theta$	26	2	0	27	1	0
T_4T_6	Δ	26	2	0	26	2	0
	Θ	28	0	0	27	1	0
	α	27	1	0	24	3	1
	β	28	0	0	23	4	1
	$\Delta + \Theta$	26	2	0	26	2	0
P_3O_1	Δ	25	2	1	26	1	1
	Θ	27	1	0	27	1	0
	α	25	3	0	26	1	1
	β	25	2	1	24	3	1
	$\Delta + \Theta$	25	2	1	27	1	0
P_4O_2	Δ	26	1	1	26	1	1
	Θ	26	2	0	25	3	0
	α	22	5	1	24	3	1
	β	23	3	2	24	4	0
	$\Delta + \Theta$	24	3	1	27	1	0
F_7T_3	Δ	27	1	0	27	1	0
	Θ	27	1	0	28	0	0
	α	27	1	0	28	0	0
	β	25	3	0	19	6	3
	$\Delta + \Theta$	27	1	0	28	0	0
F_8T_4	Δ	28	0	0	27	1	0
	Θ	26	2	0	28	0	0
	α	28	0	0	27	1	0
	β	24	3	1	22	3	3
	$\Delta + \Theta$	27	1	0	28	0	0

Note: Chi-Square and p are not significant.

NS = The number of cases with no significant departures from normality.

TABLE 15. Distribution of Z Values of Coherence and Asymmetry for Male and Female Children

		Female			Male		
		NS	.05 to .01	.01 to .001	NS	.05 to .01	.01 to .001
Coherence							
C	Δ	20	4	4	22	5	1
	Θ	23	3	2	24	3	1
	α	27	1	0	26	1	1
	β	23	3	2	26	2	0
T	Δ	26	1	1	25	2	1
	Θ	26	1	1	26	1	1
	α	26	2	0	26	1	1
	β	26	1	1	28	0	0
PO	Δ	28	0	0	28	0	0
	Θ	28	0	0	28	0	0
	α	23	3	2	27	1	0
	β	23	3	2	26	1	1
FT	Δ	27	1	0	28	0	0
	Θ	27	1	0	28	0	0
	α	27	1	0	26	1	1
	β	23	4	1	27	1	0
Power Asymmetry							
C	Δ	18	7	3	23	4	1
	Θ	27	1	0	28	0	0
	α	26	2	0	25	3	0
	β	27	1	0	26	1	1
T	Δ	28	0	0	28	0	0
	Θ	27	1	0	28	0	0
	α	25	2	1	27	1	0
	β	20	6	2	26	2	0
PO	Δ	27	1	0	26	2	0
	Θ	25	3	0	25	2	1
	α	23	3	2	23	3	2
	β	20	5	3	22	4	2
FT	Δ	25	2	1	27	1	0
	Θ	25	2	1	26	2	0
	α	26	2	0	27	1	0
	β	23	4	1	22	4	2

Note: Chi-square and *p* are not significant.

NS = The number of cases with no significant departures from normality.

TABLE 16. Distribution of Z Values of Spectral Power Estimators for Black and White Children, Age and Sex Matched

		Black			White		
		NS	.05 to .01	to .001	NS	.05 to .01	to .001
C_3C_z	Δ	28	0	0	28	0	0
	Θ	28	0	0	28	0	0
	α	27	1	0	28	0	0
	β	27	1	0	27	1	0
	$\Delta + \Theta$	28	0	0	28	0	0
C_4C_z	Δ	28	0	0	28	0	0
	Θ	28	0	0	28	0	0
	α	28	0	0	28	0	0
	β	27	1	0	27	1	0
	$\Delta + \Theta$	28	0	0	28	0	0
T_3T_5	Δ	26	2	0	28	0	0
	Θ	28	0	0	28	0	0
	α	26	2	0	25	3	0
	β	20	6	2	23	3	2
	$\Delta + \Theta$	26	2	0	27	1	0
T_4T_6	Δ	26	2	0	26	2	0
	Θ	28	0	0	27	1	0
	α	26	2	0	25	2	1
	β	26	2	0	26	1	1
	$\Delta + \Theta$	26	2	0	26	2	0
P_3O_1	Δ	26	0	2	27	1	0
	Θ	27	1	0	27	1	0
	α	24	3	1	27	1	0
	β	24	3	1	25	2	1
	$\Delta + \Theta$	25	2	1	27	1	0
P_4O_2	Δ	26	2	0	28	0	0
	Θ	25	3	0	26	2	0
	α	22	5	1	24	3	1
	β	21	5	2	26	2	0
	$\Delta + \Theta$	24	3	1	27	1	0
F_7T_3	Δ	27	1	0	27	1	0
	Θ	27	1	0	28	0	0
	α	27	1	0	27	1	0
	β	21	5	2	23	4	1
	$\Delta + \Theta$	28	0	0	27	1	0
F_8T_4	Δ	27	1	0	28	0	0
	Θ	27	1	0	27	1	0
	α	28	0	0	28	0	0
	β	20	5	3	26	1	1
	$\Delta + \Theta$	28	0	0	27	1	0

Note: Chi-square and p are not significant.
NS = The number of cases with no significant departures from normality.

TABLE 17. Distribution of Z Values of Coherence and Asymmetry for Black and White Children, Age and Sex Matched

		Black			White				
		NS	.05 to .01	.01 to .001	NS	.05 to .01	.01 to .001	χ^2	p
Coherence									
C	Δ	16	8	4	26	1	1	4.766	.05
	Θ	19	6	3	28	0	0	—	—
	α	26	1	1	27	1	0	—	—
	β	24	3	1	26	2	1	—	—
T	Δ	26	1	1	25	2	1	—	—
	Θ	28	0	0	24	2	2	—	—
	α	27	1	0	24	2	2	—	—
	β	26	1	0	28	0	0	—	—
PO	Δ	28	0	0	28	0	0	—	—
	Θ	28	0	0	27	1	0	—	—
	α	27	1	0	23	3	2	—	—
	β	26	1	1	23	3	2	—	—
FT	Δ	27	1	0	28	0	0	—	—
	Θ	27	1	0	28	0	0	—	—
	α	26	1	1	27	1	0	—	—
	β	24	3	1	26	2	0	—	—
Power Asymmetry									
C	Δ	19	6	3	22	5	1	—	—
	Θ	27	1	0	28	0	0	—	—
	α	26	2	0	25	3	0	—	—
	β	26	1	1	27	1	0	—	—
T	Δ	28	0	0	28	0	0	—	—
	Θ	28	0	0	27	1	0	—	—
	α	27	1	0	25	2	1	—	—
	β	22	6	0	24	2	2	—	—
PO	Δ	27	1	0	26	2	0	—	—
	Θ	27	1	0	23	4	1	—	—
	α	24	2	2	22	4	2	—	—
	β	20	5	3	22	4	2	—	—
FT	Δ	24	3	1	28	0	0	—	—
	Θ	27	1	0	24	3	1	—	—
	α	27	1	0	26	2	0	—	—
	β	20	6	2	25	2	1	—	—

— = not significant
NS = The number of cases with no significant departures from normality.

TABLE 18. Distribution of Z Values for 40 Spectral Power Estimators from N, SLD, and LD Children and Significant Differences between Groups

		N—Groups 1–3 ($n = 99$)				SLD—Group 6 ($n = 58$)				N v SLD	
		NS	.05	.01	.001	NS	.05	.01	.001	χ^2	p
F_7T_3	$\Delta + \Theta$	95	4	0	0	52	4	2	0	—	—
	Δ	97	2	0	0	48	7	3	0	9.944	.005
	Θ	94	5	0	0	55	1	1	1	—	—
	α	97	2	0	0	52	5	1	0	—	—
	β	88	6	5	0	47	5	6	0	—	—
F_8T_4	$\Delta + \Theta$	97	2	0	0	53	4	1	0	—	—
	Δ	98	1	0	0	52	5	1	0	5.450	.025
	Θ	97	2	0	0	53	3	2	0	—	—
	α	97	2	0	0	51	5	2	0	5.101	.025
	β	88	6	5	0	50	1	7	0	—	—
T_3T_5	$\Delta + \Theta$	99	0	0	0	51	3	4	0	9.833	.005
	Δ	99	0	0	0	48	5	4	1	15.454	.001
	Θ	97	2	0	0	53	2	3	0	—	—
	α	96	3	0	0	45	7	5	1	12.971	.001
	β	94	3	2	0	48	3	7	0	4.958	.05
T_4T_6	$\Delta + \Theta$	97	2	0	0	51	2	5	0	5.101	.025
	Δ	98	1	0	0	51	4	2	1	7.104	.01
	Θ	95	4	0	0	54	1	2	1	—	—
	α	97	2	0	0	47	5	5	1	11.687	.001
	β	91	4	4	0	47	5	6	0	—	—
C_3C_z	$\Delta + \Theta$	95	4	0	0	53	5	0	0	—	—
	Δ	94	3	2	0	53	5	0	0	—	—
	Θ	96	3	0	0	56	2	0	0	—	—
	α	98	1	0	0	53	5	0	0	3.879	.05
	β	95	2	2	0	51	7	0	0	—	—
C_4C_z	$\Delta + \Theta$	97	2	0	0	54	3	1	0	—	—
	Δ	96	3	0	0	52	6	0	0	—	—
	Θ	98	1	0	0	55	2	1	0	—	—
	α	98	1	0	0	54	3	1	0	—	—
	β	92	6	1	0	49	7	2	0	—	—
P_3O_1	$\Delta + \Theta$	97	2	0	0	45	6	7	0	15.321	.001
	Δ	97	1	1	0	47	3	6	2	11.687	.001
	Θ	97	1	1	0	48	5	5	0	9.944	.005
	α	95	2	2	0	44	8	3	3	10.796	.005
	β	93	4	2	0	51	4	3	0	—	—
P_4O_2	$\Delta + \Theta$	97	2	0	0	45	6	7	0	15.321	.001
	Δ	97	2	0	0	47	4	6	1	11.687	.001
	Θ	96	3	0	0	47	8	2	1	9.557	.005
	α	95	1	3	0	47	6	4	1	7.780	.01
	β	92	5	2	0	51	4	3	0	—	—

Note: See table 11 for NS, .05, .01, and .001.
— = Not significant.

LD—Group 7 (n = 55)				N v LD		SLD + LD (n = 113)				N v (SLD + LD)	
NS	.05	.01	.001	χ^2	p	NS	.05	.01	.001	χ^2	p
47	6	2	0	4.067	.05	99	10	4	0	—	—
45	6	1	3	10.702	.005	93	13	4	3	12.313	.001
52	3	0	0	—	—	107	4	1	1	—	—
46	7	2	0	8.911	.005	98	12	3	0	7.600	.01
47	4	4	0	—	—	94	9	10	0	—	—
48	6	1	0	5.549	.025	101	10	2	0	5.009	.05
49	3	2	1	5.867	.025	101	8	3	1	6.878	.01
50	3	1	1	—	—	103	6	3	1	—	—
51	2	1	1	—	—	102	7	3	1	4.198	.05
44	5	6	0	—	—	94	6	13	0	—	—
49	5	1	0	8.315	.005	100	8	5	0	10.217	.005
48	5	2	0	10.430	.005	96	10	6	1	14.217	.001
50	2	3	0	—	—	103	4	6	0	—	—
46	6	3	0	6.991	.01	91	13	8	1	12.174	.001
47	4	4	0	—	—	95	7	11	0	5.381	.025
49	4	2	0	4.011	.05	100	6	7	0	5.849	.025
52	2	1	0	—	—	103	6	3	1	5.095	.025
51	2	2	0	—	—	105	3	4	1	—	—
46	7	2	0	8.911	.005	93	12	7	1	12.313	.001
46	6	3	0	—	—	93	11	9	0	—	—
50	4	1	0	—	—	103	9	1	0	—	—
45	6	4	0	5.522	.025	98	11	4	0	—	—
52	2	1	0	—	—	108	4	1	0	—	—
48	6	1	0	7.621	.01	101	11	1	0	6.878	.01
49	5	1	0	—	—	100	12	1	0	—	—
50	2	3	0	—	—	104	5	4	0	—	—
44	9	2	0	10.352	.005	96	15	2	0	7.564	.01
51	4	0	0	—	—	106	6	1	0	—	—
51	4	0	0	—	—	105	7	1	0	—	—
50	2	3	0	—	—	99	9	5	0	—	—
41	12	2	0	18.415	.001	86	18	9	0	19.569	.001
44	5	5	1	12.554	.001	91	8	11	3	14.313	.001
46	6	2	1	8.911	.005	94	11	7	1	11.336	.001
46	6	3	0	4.192	.05	90	14	6	3	9.487	.005
49	4	2	0	—	—	100	8	5	0	—	—
46	3	6	0	8.911	.005	91	9	13	0	14.313	.001
45	5	3	2	10.702	.005	92	9	9	3	13.305	.001
48	5	2	0	3.995	.05	95	13	4	1	8.446	.005
42	9	4	0	11.902	.001	89	15	8	1	12.157	.001
46	8	1	0	—	—	97	12	4	0	—	—

TABLE 19. Distribution of Z Values for 32 Measures of Coherence and Power Asymmetry in Data from N, SLD, and LD Children and Significant Differences between Groups

		N—Groups 1–3 (n = 99)				SLD—Group 6 (n = 58)				N v SLD	
		NS	.05	.01	.001	NS	.05	.01	.001	χ^2	p
Coherence											
$FT(F_7T_3 \, \nu \, F_8T_4)$	Δ	94	1	2	2	50	1	5	2	—	—
	Θ	92	4	2	1	53	3	1	1	—	—
	α	97	1	1	0	54	4	0	0	—	—
	β	92	5	1	1	58	0	0	0	—	—
$T(T_3T_5 \, \nu \, T_4T_6)$	Δ	91	2	3	3	52	1	4	1	—	—
	Θ	90	6	1	2	54	2	2	0	—	—
	α	95	2	2	0	58	0	0	0	—	—
	β	94	4	1	0	55	0	2	1	—	—
$C(C_3C_z \, \nu \, C_4C_z)$	Δ	94	2	3	0	49	5	0	4	—	—
	Θ	92	5	2	0	50	4	4	0	—	—
	α	92	5	1	1	47	4	6	1	3.993	.05
	β	94	4	0	1	58	0	0	0	—	—
$PO(P_3O_1 \, \nu \, P_4O_2)$	Δ	94	5	0	0	53	2	1	2	—	—
	Θ	96	2	0	1	55	1	0	2	—	—
	α	93	4	2	0	53	2	3	0	—	—
	β	96	3	0	0	53	4	0	1	—	—
Power asymmetry											
$FT(F_7T_3 \, \nu \, F_8T_4)$ $200\frac{L-R}{L+R}$	Δ	90	6	3	0	43	9	6	0	6.701	.01
	Θ	91	6	2	0	52	1	5	0	—	—
	α	91	4	4	0	52	5	1	0	—	—
	β	95	1	3	0	54	2	2	0	—	—
$T(T_3T_5 \, \nu \, T_4T_6)$	Δ	96	3	0	0	54	2	2	0	—	—
	Θ	95	3	1	0	56	2	0	0	—	—
	α	94	4	1	0	56	2	0	0	—	—
	β	89	7	3	0	52	3	3	0	—	—
$C(C_3C_z \, \nu \, C_4C_z)$	Δ	94	5	0	0	48	4	6	0	4.958	.05
	Θ	89	7	3	0	54	3	1	0	—	—
	α	90	7	2	0	55	1	2	0	—	—
	β	94	3	2	0	56	0	2	0	—	—
$PO(P_3O_1 \, \nu \, P_4O_2)$	Δ	96	2	1	0	51	3	4	0	—	—
	Θ	95	2	2	0	48	4	6	0	6.306	.025
	α	92	5	2	0	49	5	4	0	—	—
	β	93	4	2	0	51	3	4	0	—	—
Total		2,980	124	52	12	1,683	82	76	15		

Note: See table 11 for NS, .05, .01, .001.
— = Not significant.

LD—Group 7 (n = 55)				N v LD		SLD + LD (n = 113)				N v (SLD + LD)	
NS	.05	.01	.001	χ^2	p	NS	.05	.01	.001	χ^2	p
49	3	0	3	—	—	99	4	5	5	—	—
47	4	3	1	—	—	100	7	4	2	—	—
54	0	1	0	—	—	108	4	1	0	—	—
53	1	0	1	—	—	111	1	0	1	—	—
49	3	1	2	—	—	101	4	5	3	—	—
51	2	0	2	—	—	105	4	2	2	—	—
54	1	0	0	—	—	112	1	0	0	—	—
52	2	0	1	—	—	107	2	2	2	—	—
47	4	1	3	—	—	96	9	1	7	4.643	.05
49	4	1	1	—	—	99	8	5	1	—	—
53	1	1	0	—	—	100	5	7	1	—	—
54	0	1	0	—	—	112	0	1	0	—	—
47	1	4	3	—	—	100	3	5	5	—	—
49	2	2	2	—	—	104	3	2	4	—	—
48	3	1	3	—	—	101	5	4	3	—	—
47	4	0	4	5.439	.025	100	8	0	5	4.284	.05
42	6	7	0	4.979	.05	85	15	13	0	7.958	.005
46	6	3	0	—	—	98	7	8	0	—	—
53	1	1	0	—	—	105	6	2	0	—	—
47	5	3	0	4.067	.05	101	7	5	0	—	—
53	1	1	0	—	—	107	3	3	0	—	—
51	2	2	0	—	—	107	4	2	0	—	—
53	0	2	0	—	—	109	2	2	0	—	—
48	3	4	0	—	—	100	6	7	0	—	—
50	3	2	0	—	—	98	7	8	0	—	—
50	2	3	0	—	—	104	5	4	0	—	—
48	3	4	0	—	—	103	4	6	0	—	—
53	2	0	0	—	—	109	2	2	0	—	—
51	1	3	0	—	—	102	4	7	0	—	—
43	9	3	0	10.169	.005	91	13	9	0	10.284	.005
47	5	3	0	—	—	96	10	7	0	—	—
47	5	3	0	—	—	98	8	7	0	—	—
1,585	89	60	26			3,260	171	136	41		

TABLE 20. Distribution of Z Values of 40 Spectral Power Estimators in N, SLD, LD and Combined SLD plus LD Groups Probability level of Z Values

Group	n	Total Measures	$p > .05$	$.05 \leq p > .01$	$.01 \leq p > .001$	$p \leq$
N	99	3,960	3,827 (96.6)	103 (2.6)	30 (0.76)	0 (0
SLD	58	2,320	2,010 (86.6)	176 (7.59)	120 (5.17)	14 (0
LD	55	2,200	1,906 (86.6)	195 (8.86)	89 (4.0)	10 (0
SLD + LD	113	4,520	3,916 (86.6)	371 (8.21)	209 (4.62)	24 (0

Note: Parenthetical values show the percent of total measures in each range.

TABLE 21. Chi-squared Estimates of Significance of Differences between Distributions of Neurometric EEG Measures in N, SLD, LD, and Combined SLD plus LD Groups, by Derivation and by Measure

		Fronto-temporal L	R	Temporal L	R	Central L	R	Parieto-Occipital L	R
N v SLD	Δ + Θ	*.005*	*.025*	*.005*	*.025*	—	—	*.001*	*.001*
	Δ	—	—	*.001*	.01	—	—	*.001*	*.001*
	Θ	—	—	—	—	—	—	*.005*	*.005*
	α	—	.025	*.001*	*.001*	*.05*	—	*.005*	*.01*
	β	—	—	.05	—	—	—	—	—
	COH	—		—		.05(α)		—	
	PA Δ	*.01*		—		.05		—	
	PA Θ	—		—		—		.025	
N v LD	Δ + Θ	.05	.025	*.005*	.05	—	—	*.001*	*.005*
	Δ	.005	.025	*.005*	—	.025	.005	*.001*	*.005*
	Θ	—	—	—	—	—	—	*.005*	.05
	α	.005	—	*.01*	*.005*	*.01*	—	*.05*	*.001*
	β	—	—	—	—	—	—	—	—
	COH	—		—		—		.025(β)	
	PA Δ	*.05*		—		—		—	
	PA Θ	.05		—		—		*.005*	
N v (SLD + LD)	Δ + Θ	—	.05	.005	.025	—	—	.001	.001
	Δ	.001	.01	.001	.025	—	.01	.001	.001
	Θ	—	—	—	—	—	—	.001	.005
	α	.01	.05	.001	.001	.01	—	.005	.001
	β	—	—	.025	—	—	—	—	—
	COH	—		—		.05(Δ)		.05(β)	
	PAΔ	.005		—		—		—	
	PAΘ	—		—		—		.005	

N = n = 99
SLD = n = 58
LD = n = 55
COH = Coherence
PA = Power Asymmetry
— = Not significant.
Italics = Measures on which both SLD and LD differed significantly from normal.

TABLE 22. Neurometric Replication Studies

Country	Category	Age Range	n	Agreement on Univariate Features
Normative Equations				
United States[1]	N	6–16	306	31 of 32 slopes same
Sweden	N	1–21	342	31 of 32 slopes same
Replications				
Barbados	N	7–12	129	4.0% false positives
United States[2]	N	10–16	57	5.3% false positives
Cuba	N	7–11	256	30 of 32 slopes same
Mexico	N	7–12	28	30 of 32 slopes same
Venezuela	N	7–12	26	31 of 32 slopes same
Sensitivities				
United States[1]	N	6–16	153	11% correct positives
	SLD	6–16	159	49% correct positives
	LD	6–16	139	61% correct positives
	MR	6–16	46	72% correct positives
United States[2]	N	10–16	57	5.3% correct positives
	Dyslexic	10–16	56	10.5% correct positives
Germany	N	10–13	25	4% correct positives
	LD	10–13	11	55% correct positives
	MR	10–13	14	65% correct positives
Cuba	N	7–11	160	2.5% correct positives
	MR	7–11	127	81% correct positives
Mexico	Risk and Disadvantaged	7–12	28	13 of 32 slopes different
Mexico	Risk and low SES	7–12	30	9 of 32 slopes different
Venezuela	Risk and low SES	4–12	55	9 of 32 slopes different

Sources: Barbados: Ahn et al. 1980; Cuba: Alvarez, Pascual, and Valdes 1987; Germany: Gasser et al. 1983a, b; Mexico: Harmony et al. 1987a; Sweden: Matousek and Peterson 1973; United States: (1) John et al. 1983, (2) Yingling et al. 1986; Venezuela: Ramus Reported in Harmony et al. 1987a.

TABLE 23. Influence of Cultural Factors, Incidence of Abnormal Neurometric Results

Group	Category	Risk	Total n	% Abnormal	% Maturational Lag
I	Grade level	Absent	51	15	12
		Present	55	18	18
II	One year below	Absent	38	11	13
	grade level	Present	44	25	23
III	Consistent	Absent	7	0	0
	failure	Present	19	21	26
IV	Illiterate	Absent	6	50	17
		Present	8	75	50

TABLE 24. Distribution of Significant Differences between N and LD Grand Average EPs for Every Visual EP Item as a Function of 10/20 Lend and Component Latency

Latency Intervals (MS)

P_z

80	100	120	140	160	180	200	220	240	260	280	300	320	340	360	380	400	420	440	460	480	500	520
							49	51														
							48*	50														
							47*	49														
							46**	78														
54							45**	77*														
48							44	76*														
47**							43	71				55							53			
41*	60			57*			39*	70*		46*		46*	44*		45**				47	48		
40	59	53	72	51*			33	69				40*	41*		39*	81	61	45*	70*	70*	40	74
87				50*			80	64		74		82	99	75	79	66	56*	81	67		40	72*
								67		43	53											

P_3

80	100	120	140	160	180	200	220	240	260	280	300	320	340	360	380	400	420	440	460	480	500	520
									57													
48*									78**													
47*									77**													
46**									76													
45								52	75			55	50		52			53				
44								51**	70**			47	44*	48	51*			69				
								49	69**			46*	43*	45*	41							
41**				57*				39**	64*	87		46*	42*	45**	39**			45	64*			74
40				50				63	62	74	53	40**	72	79	33			78	62			70*

P₄

47	60		47	43		57		61	43*	45	56	
46*	77	57	41*	42	57	51		40*	42*	41**	52	
44	71	51	40**	39**	51	99		66	82**		46	
		50*	33**	71	99	78*					44	53
		45*	80	67	78*	77**					40	
				64	77**	76**					39	45
					76**	75					33	99
					75	70**					79	67
					70**	69**						64
					69**	68						72
					68	62*	74	55				70*
					62*							74

T₅

48				59	83	61*	48	45	56	61**
47	57	55	60	56	75*	44	47	41	52	52
46	36	43	59	53	70*	43	46*	72	51	78
45	75	30	65	51*	69**	33	40**	65	39	66*
44		55		39	63	68	68	62	73	65
41	39	54		81	62*					64*
		36*		78**					53	80
				77**						69
				76**						67
				72						
				67*						
				64*						

T₆

61			60	40	51*	52	56*	59
47	43		59	39*	77*	72	52	81
46	99*	76	57	78	70	66*	41	70
41	93		43	76*	62	65	65	67
				69			39	64
							66	
							61	
							99**	
							64	72

Table 24 continued on next page.

Table 24—*Continued*

Latency Intervals (MS)

	80	100	120	140	160	180	200	220	240	260	280	300	320	340	360	380	400	420	440	460	480	500	520
O_1	54																						
	50																						
	48*																						
	47*								78														
	46**								77														
	45			57					76														
	44			43						70**				45	52*								
	41**			36				57		69**				41	90								
	40*	78		30	52			49*		68		53	53	40**	79	56		64	30	69	60		
	39	76	55	93	93	93	56	67		62	60	43	51**	33	65	53							
O_2	50*																						
	49																						
	48						59																
	47						55																
	46						39		50														
	45						33		77														
	44						81		70*					41									
	41						80		69*					40*					99				
	40						71		68*					81									
	78	76	93	43	52	93	67	51*	62					75	52					67			

Note: Entries with no asterisk are significant at the .05 level, one asterisk at the .01 level and two asterisks at the .001 level.

TABLE 25. Significant Changes in N-LD Grand Average EP Waveshapes, Distribution of Likelihood Ratios for Mahalanobis Distances, and Both Measures at $p < .01$, for All Leads of 10/20 System

EP Item	Item No.	Grand Avg EP N	Grand Avg EP LD	Mahalanobis N	Mahalanobis LD	Fp1	Fp2	F3	F4	C3	C4	P3	P4	O1	O2	F7	F8	T3	T4	T5	T6	Fz	Cz	Pz	Across Leads	Total D	Total M	Total B	Grand Total by Item
Predicting temporal order items																													
Regular flash	30	63	32	15	35					M				M	M										M	0	4	0	4
Regular click	31	63	34	16	35					D	M									D			D			3	1	0	4
Regular tap	32	63	33	15	32		D				D		D						D		D	D	B			6	0	1	7
Random flash	33	55	25	13	30	D					D				D									D		4	0	0	4
Random click	34	55	25	14	29		M				M				M	D										1	2	0	3
Random tap	35	54	25	13	28			M		M	M	B	M	B	B				B			M	B		M	0	6	5	11
Random-regular flash	36	44	25	13	29				M	M	M	M	M				M		D		D				M	2	7	0	9
Random-regular click	37	55	25	14	28	D						D	D					D	D	D						6	0	0	6
Random-regular tap	38	54	25	13	26			D				D						D				D		D		5	0	0	5
Habituation-rehabituation																													
Habituation 1 (H1)	39	55	22	10	24	M				D	B	D	D	M	M	B	B	D			D		B	D	M	6	4	4	14
Habituation 2 (H2)	40	55	22	10	24					B	B	B	B	B		B	D	D	D	D			B	B	M	4	1	8	13
Habituation 3 (H3)	41	55	22	10	24					M	D	D	D	B	B	D	D	D					D	B	M	7	2	3	12
Habituation 4 (H4)	42	55	22	10	24	D			M	M		D	D	B				D						D	M	5	3	1	9

Table 25 continued on next page.

Table 25—Continued

EP Item	Item No.	Grand Average EP N	Grand Average EP LD	Grand Mahalanobis Distance N	Grand Mahalanobis Distance LD	Fp1	Fp2	F3	F4	C3	C4	P3	P4	O1	O2	F7	F8	T3	T4	T5	T6	Fz	Cz	Pz	Across Leads	Total D	Total M	Total B	Grand Total by Item
Habituation 5 (H5)	43	55	22	10	24	D				M	D	D	D	M	M	D	D		B					M	M	6	5	1	12
Rehabituation 1 (R1)	44	52	18	10	23						D	D		D			D						D	D		5	0	0	5
Rehabituation 2 (R2)	45	52	18	10	23				D		B	D	B	D		D	D	D		D			D	D		9	0	2	11
Rehabituation 3 (R3)	46	52	18	10	23				D	B	B	B	D	D		D	D			D			D	B		7	0	4	11
Rehabituation 4 (R4)	47	52	18	10	23			D	D	D	D	D		D		D	D	B		D			D			10	0	1	11
Rehabituation 5 (R5)	48	52	18	10	23			D	D	B	D	D	D	D		D	D	D	D	D			D	D		13	0	1	14
Rate of habituation																													
H1 – H2	49	55	22	10	24									D								M				1	1	0	2
H1 – H3	50	55	22	10	24								D	D	D									B		3	0	1	4
H1 – H4	51	55	22	10	24					D	B	D	M	D	D		M		D	D			D	D		8	2	1	11
H1 – H5	52	55	22	10	24			D	D																	2	0	0	2
R1 – R2	53	52	18	10	23																					0	0	0	0
R1 – R3	54	52	18	10	23	D		M																		1	1	0	2
R1 – R4	55	52	18	10	23	D																M				1	1	0	2
R1 – R5	56	52	18	10	23	D														D				D		3	0	0	3

Memory of habituation

Item	No.					Individual responses	D	M	B	Total
H1 – R1	57	52	18	10	22	D M M B	1	2	1	4
H2 – R2	58	52	18	10	22	M M M	0	3	0	3
H3 – R3	59	52	18	10	22	D D	2	0	0	2
H4 – R4	60	52	18	10	22	D	1	0	0	1
H5 – R5	61	52	18	10	22	D D D D D	5	0	0	5

Sensory acuity and contrast

Item	No.					Individual responses	D	M	B	Total
Blank	62	55	38	17	44	M M D M M M D M M	2	7	0	9
7 lines/in.	63	54	38	17	44	M M M M	0	4	0	4
27 lines/in.	64	52	27	17	44	M D M M D M	2	4	0	6
Blank—7 lines/in.	65	54	38	17	44	M M M M M	0	5	0	5
Blank—27 lines/in.	66	52	27	17	44	D D D D D	5	0	0	5

Perception of geometric forms

Item	No.					Individual responses	D	M	B	Total
Lg. square (S)	67	48	32	16	38	M D D	2	1	0	3
Sm. square (s)	68	47	32	15	37	D D B D	3	0	1	4
Lg. diamond (D)	69	47	31	15	35	D B B D D M D D	5	1	2	8
Sm. diamond (d)	70	47	29	15	33	M D B D D B D D D M D	8	2	1	11
S – s	71	47	32	15	37	M M M M D M M M M M M M M M	1	13	0	14
D – d	72	47	29	15	33	M M M D M M D M D	3	6	0	9
S – D	73	47	31	15	35	M M M D M M M M M M B M	1	10	1	12
s – d	74	47	29	15	33	M B M M D B	1	3	2	6

Perception of letters

Item	No.					Individual responses	D	M	B	Total
b	75	52	32	15	37	M M M M D	1	4	0	5
d	76	31	26	15	32	D D D D D D D D D	9	0	0	9
p	77	25	25	14	31	D B D B D B D B D M M M	5	3	4	12
q	78	24	25	14	31	D D B D D M	5	1	0	6

Table 25 continued on next page.

Table 25—*Continued*

EP Item	Item No.	EP N	EP LD	Mahal. N	Mahal. LD	Fp1	Fp2	F3	F4	C3	C4	P3	P4	O1	O2	F7	F8	T3	T4	T5	T6	Fz	Cz	Pz	Across Leads	Total D	Total M	Total B	Grand Total by Item
$b - d$	79	31	26	15	32						D		M								M	M	D		M	2	4	0	6
$p - q$	80	24	25	14	31					M					M		M									0	3	0	3
$b - p$	81	25	25	14	31	D					D	D						M	M							3	2	0	5
$d - q$	82	24	25	14	31		M	B	D	D	D		M	M			B			M	D		D	D	M	6	5	2	13
$b - q$	83	24	25	14	31						D		M							D	M					2	2	0	4
Figure-ground relations—visual figure																													
Defocused video and flash	84	32	26	7	26	B	M	M		B		M		D	M	M		B	M	M					M	1	8	3	12
Defocused video and click	85	32	26	7	26	M	M	M	M				M			M	M		D	M	M		B		M	1	10	1	12
Defocused video and tap	86	32	26	7	26				M				D	D	D			D	M	D		M				5	3	0	8
Focused video and flash	87	53	29	12	24	M	M	M		M	M			M	M	M	B		M						M	0	10	1	11
Focused video and click	88	52	29	12	24	D				D	D	D		D			D	D	D				D	D		10	0	0	10
Focused video and tap	89	53	29	12	24	M		M		D	D	B	D	D	D		D	D	B	D	M	M	B	B	M	8	5	4	17

Measure	No.					Markers (reading order)	D	B	M	Total
Visual-visual interaction	90	32	26	6	22	D D B D D D D D D	8	0	1	9
Visual-auditory interaction	91	32	26	6	22	D D D D D D M	6	1	0	7
Visual-tactile interaction	92	32	26	6	20	D D D D D D D D D	7	0	0	7

Figure-ground relations—auditory figure

Measure	No.					Markers (reading order)	D	B	M	Total
Music + flash	93	50	22	8	21	D D D D D B M B	3	1	2	6
Music + click	94	50	22	8	21	D B D D D D D D D D D D	10	0	1	11
Music + tap	95	50	22	8	21	D D D D M D D D D D D	11	1	0	12
Auditory-visual interaction	96	50	22	7	21	D D D D D D B D D D	10	0	1	11
Auditory-auditory interaction	97	50	22	8	21	D D D D D D D D D D D D D D D D	14	0	0	14
Auditory-tactile interaction	98	50	22	8	20	M	0	1	0	1

Sensory-sensory conditioning[+]

Measure	No.			Markers
Flash before	99	25	3	
F + C pairing				
Click before	100	25	3	
F + C pairing				
Tap before	101	25	3	
F + C pairing				
Flash + click pairing	102	24	3	
Flash after	103	23	3	# # # # # #
F + C pairing				

Table 25 continued next page.

Table 25—Continued

EP Item	Item No.	Grand Average EP N	LD	Mahalanobis Distance N	LD	Fp1	Fp2	F3	F4	C3	C4	P3	P4	O1	O2	F7	F8	T3	T4	T5	T6	Fz	Cz	Pz	Across Leads	D	M	B	Grand Total by Item
Click after F + C pairing	104	23	3					#	#	#	#						#	#	#				#	#					
Tap after F + C pairing	105	23	3				#	#	#	#	#									#	#	#	#	#					
Click + flash pairing	106	21	3																										
Flash after C + F pairing	107	16	3						#			#							#										
Click after C + F pairing	108	16	3					#	#	#	#			#	#		#	#		#	#	#	#	#					
Tap after C + F pairing	109	16	3						#			#	#	#	#	#	#	#	#	#	#	#							
Flash (after-before F + C)	110	23	3																										
Click (after-before F + C)	111	23	3																										
Tap (after-before F + C)	112	23	3																										
Flash (after-before C + F)	113	16	3																										

Click (after-before C + F)	114	16	3			
Tap (after before C + F)	115	16	3			

Totals

Total significant N-LD t-test (D)	10	2	7	7	20	18	26	16	18	9	8	18	24	18	22	13	12	17	22	—	287	—
Total significant Mahalanobis distance (M)	3	5	12	9	13	7	4	10	9	12	4	10	4	6	7	5	10	8	5	22	—	165 —
Total significant N-LD and Mahalanobis distance (B)	1	0	1	1	6	7	5	6	5	2	1	3	8	4	2	0	0	3	8	—	—	63
Grand total by lead	14	7	20	17	39	32	35	32	32	23	13	31	36	28	31	18	22	28	35	22	—	—

Grand total significant by lead × item = 515
Total number leads × items = 1,380

Note: For each item, the size of the sample of N and LD children used to construct the Grand Average EP is indicated, as is the size of the sample of each group evaluated by computation of the Mahalanobis distance. The size of the sample of normal children used to define the normal hyperellipsoid can be obtained by subtracting, for every item, the number of normal children evaluated by Mahalanobis distance computations from the number included in the construction of the Grand Average. For most items, EPs from 25 to 48 normal children were used to define the hyperellipsoid. When the available sample of data from normal children was too small (items 75–83), the sample size of normal children used for this purpose became as small as 10. On most items the number of LD children does not exactly correspond for the two kinds of computation. Usually, this reflects the fact that NB testing of additional LD children, later evaluated by the Mahalanobis distance, took place after computation of the Grand Average EPs, variances, and N-LD difference waves based upon a smaller group. In a few cases, data on items 84–98 were inconvenient to retrieve for some LD children at the time when the Mahalanobis distances were computed (technical problems) and were omitted from the sample.

D means that the N-LD difference wave was significant at any latency, with $p < .01$.

M means that the distribution of the Mahalanobis distance in the N and LD test groups was significantly different with $p < .01$.

B means that *both* the N-LD difference wave and the Mahalanobis difference were significantly different, with $p < .01$.

Empty cells indicate no significant change.

+No hyperellipsoid computed for these items

Significant change ($p < .01$) in waveshape of N group, but LD sample too small to compute N-LD difference

TABLE 26. Classification Accuracy of N and LD Children by the Mahalanobis Distance, and the Significance of Differences between the Distribution of this Measure in N and LD Children, as Assessed by Chi-Squared Analysis

Item No.	% N Classified Erroneously as False Positives	% LD Classified Correctly	χ^2	p
62	5.9	40.9	6.700	.001
63	11.8	30.2	—	NS
64	5.9	20.4	—	NS
67	6.2	26.3	—	NS
68	0.0	10.8	—	NS
69	6.7	14.3	—	NS
70	6.7	45.4	5.345	.025
75	6.7	27.6	—	NS
76	0.0	0.0	—	NS
77	7.1	35.5	2.645	NS
78	7.1	16.1	—	NS
30	13.3	20.0	—	NS
33	7.7	10.0	—	NS
84	0.0	53.8	4.528	.05
87	0.0	45.8	5.907	.025
93	12.5	28.6	—	NS
39	0.0	32.0	2.532	NS
40	0.0	20.0	—	NS
41	0.0	36.0	3.145	NS
42	0.0	44.0	4.537	.05
43	0.0	36.0	3.145	NS
44	0.0	8.7	—	NS
45	0.0	4.3	—	NS
46	0.0	34.8	2.983	NS
65	0.0	20.4	—	NS
66	0.0	4.5	—	NS
71	0.0	21.6	—	NS
72	6.7	33.3	2.618	NS
73	0.0	13.9	—	NS
74	6.7	33.3	2.618	NS
79	13.3	28.1	—	NS
80	14.3	22.6	—	NS
81	21.4	29.0	—	NS
82	7.1	32.2	2.074	NS
83	0.0	9.7	—	NS
36	0.0	10.3	—	NS

TABLE 26—*Continued*

Item No.	% N Classified Erroneously as False Positives	% LD Classified Correctly	χ^2	p
31	12.5	14.3	—	NS
34	14.3	27.6	—	NS
85	0.0	30.8	1.415	NS
94	0.0	42.8	3.171	NS
32	6.2	28.1	—	NS
35	0.0	25.0	—	NS
86	0.0	57.7	5.260	.025
89	7.7	63.6	8.283	.005
95	0.0	40.0	2.734	NS
All conditions	10.0	36.5	3.723	NS
All challenges	5.0	25.0	2.522	NS

TABLE 27. Accuracy of Discrimination between N and LD Groups for Each 10/20 Lead and EP Items

Item No.	Sample Size N	LD	F_{P1}	F_{P2}	F_3	F_4	C_3	C_4	P_3	P_4	O_1	O_2	F_7	F_8	T_3	T_4	T_5	T_6	F_z	C_z	P_z	All Leads
Predicting temporal order																						
30	15	35						6/11			6/14	13/20								6/17		
31	16	35						12/14														
32	16	32																				
33	13	30													6/28							
34	14	29		14/25															14/27			
35	13	28			7/17		15/21		7/25	0/25	7/35	0/25			7/57	0/10	7/28				0/21	15/32
36	13	29				0/17	7/17	7/6	7/24					0/10	0/24							0/6
37	14	28																				
38	13	26																				
Habituation-rehabituation																						
39	10	24	10/22					0/20			20/29	0/33		0/29		0/25				0/16		0/16
40	10	24					10/54	10/37	0/20		10/29	20/37			10/20					10/29	10/54	0/29
41	10	24					0/29	0/37			10/41	10/29										10/20
42	10	24						10/37			0/37	10/45										0/16
43	10	24						10/29			10/37	10/25				0/29					0/20	0/20
44	10	23																				
45	10	23						10/26								10/21						
46	10	23						0/30	20/34	10/26					0/34							
47	10	23																			0/34	
48	10	23						20/26														

Rate of habituation

49	10	24							20/29		10/25	
50	10	24										
51	10	24		10/45	30/16							
52	10	24										
53	10	23										
54	10	23	0/26				20/20	20/34				
55	10	23										
56	10	23										

Memory of habituation

57	10	22								0/9	10/13	
58	10	22		0/36	10/22							
59	10	22					20/13	20/18				
60	10	22										
61	10	22										

Sensory acuity and contrast

62	17	44	11/18	5/40			17/18		0/9	11/34	5/11	5/25
63	17	44		5/13	11/11		11/29					5/22
64	17	44	5/11	5/20	0/16					0/18	0/6	
65	17	44	0/18	0/13	5/20							
66	17	44	0/4									

Perception of geometric forms

67	16	38			6/26							
68	15	37			0/10	6/14	0/14					
69	15	35	6/45	6/21	6/14							
70	15	33		3/24						20/8	13/21	
71	15	37	0/16	0/8	13/13	6/40	13/29	0/10	6/18	6/8	6/21	6/13	0/21	6/27	6/15

Table 27 continued on next page.

TABLE 27—Continued

Item No.	Sample Size N	LD	F_{p1}	F_{p2}	F_3	F_4	C_3	C_4	P_3	P_4	O_1	O_2	F_7	F_8	T_3	T_4	T_5	T_6	F_z	C_z	P_z	All Leads
72	15	33				6/15	6/30							6/15	6/24	20/21						0/12
73	15	35			0/11	6/14	13/17	0/14	6/25			6/11		0/8			6/17		6/20	0/8		6/20
74	15	33				6/12	6/33		13/18								6/24					6/12
Perception of letters																						
75	15	37		13/17					6/21	6/13		6/21										
76	15	32																				
77	14	31			7/35		7/22			0/6		7/29			21/32		0/16					14/22
78	14	31																			7/16	
79	15	32								13/28								13/15	20/21			6/18
80	14	31					7/16					14/12		0/12								
81	14	31														7/16	14/25					
82	14	31		0/6	14/19					14/22	7/29			7/16			7/19					7/16
83	14	31																7/12		0/9		
Figure-ground relations—visual figure																						
84	7	26	0/53	0/23	0/26		14/23			14/38		14/42	14/34	14/38	14/42	0/34	28/50		28/38	14/15		14/53
85	7	26		14/42	14/46	42/38	0/15			14/53			28/50	14/38								14/50
86	7	26				28/42										0/57			0/42			
87	12	24	8/25		25/41		16/45	8/12			16/29	8/33	16/25	16/37			8/20		16/20			0/45
88	12	24																				
89	12	24	7/22		7/36				23/36							7/63		15/22	7/40	15/22	15/54	15/40
90	6	22								0/18	0/22											
91	6	22																				
92	6	20																				

Figure-ground relations—Auditory figure

93	8	21				0/11	12/28 25/42
94	8	21	0/42				
95	8	21		0/40	14/33		
96	7	21					
97	8	21			0/25		
98	8	20					

TABLE 28. Distribution of Significant Z Values for EP Features Summed across Leads for N and LD Groups on Every EP Item of the Core NB

EP Item	Item No.	Group	6 .01	6 .001	1A .01	1A .001	1B .01	1B .001	2A .01	2A .001	2B .01	2B .001
Regular	31	I	16	2	6	0	2	0	0	0	0	0
click		II	20	8	27	6	18	4	16	0	6	0
		III	2	0	3	0	3	1	2	0	3	1
		IV	16	4	14	2	7	2	5	0	7	0
Blank	62	I	35	5	3	0	10	0	3	0	8	0
flash		II	76	14	22	4	24	8	8	2	2	4
		III	1	0	2	0	2	0	1	0	4	0
		IV	37	11	5	0	7	0	11	0	5	2
7 line/in.	63	I	15	2	18	0	8	0	16	2	5	0
		II	69	14	37	8	12	10	22	4	16	0
		III	4	0	2	0	2	0	0	0	3	0
		IV	41	11	27	4	21	2	23	5	18	0
27 line/in.	64	I	8	0	5	0	8	2	3	0	2	0
		II	24	10	16	2	24	6	10	2	6	2
		III	1	0	3	0	3	0	4	0	1	0
		IV	30	5	7	0	29	7	4	2	14	2
b	75	I	8	0	8	0	6	0	3	0	2	0
		II	47	12	14	6	12	6	8	0	6	4
		III	0	0	5	0	3	0	3	0	3	0
		IV	54	11	20	4	18	11	9	2	16	4
d	76	I	0	0	2	2	13	0	3	0	10	0
		II	24	10	10	4	8	2	2	0	12	0
		III	0	0	6	0	1	0	1	1	3	0
		IV	27	4	11	2	14	0	7	0	5	0
All		I	XX	XX	7	0	8	0	5	0	6	0
		II	XX	XX	21	5	17	6	11	1	8	2
		III	XX	XX	4	0	3	0	2	0	3	0
		IV	XX	XX	14	2	16	4	10	1	11	1

6 = Mahalanobis distance from hyperellipsoid, 100–260 ms
1A = Log maximum signal to noise, negative Z values, 300–500 ms
1B = Log maximum signal to noise, negative Z values, 0–500 ms
2A = Log mean power, negative Z values, 300–500 ms
2B = Log mean power, negative Z values, 0–500 ms
3A = Log mean power, positive Z values, 300–500 ms
3B = Log mean power, positive Z values, 0–500 ms
4A = Log mean difference power, positive Z values, 300–500 ms
4B = Log mean difference power, positive Z values, 0–500 ms

	3A		3B		4A		4B		5A		5B		Total	
	.01	.001	.01	.001	.01	.001	.01	.001	.01	.001	.01	.001	.01	.001
	0	0	0	0	2	0	0	0	0	0	2	0	1	0
	4	2	6	2	12	0	14	4	2	0	4	0	11	2
	1	0	2	2	2	0	2	0	1	1	0	1	2	0
	0	0	4	0	5	0	11	4	0	0	2	0	6	1
	3	0	5	0	0	0	2	0	0	0	0	0	3	0
	6	0	6	0	6	0	6	0	4	2	2	0	9	2
	1	0	1	0	1	0	1	0	1	0	1	1	1	0
	2	2	7	2	0	0	0	0	2	0	2	2	4	1
	2	0	5	0	0	0	2	0	3	0	15	2	6	0
	8	2	4	2	4	0	6	0	10	0	6	2	13	3
	0	0	0	0	0	0	0	0	2	1	2	1	1	0
	0	4	2	4	0	0	4	0	5	0	9	2	11	2
	0	0	0	0	2	0	2	0	2	0	0	0	3	0
	6	12	8	8	0	4	8	6	2	0	2	0	8	4
	0	0	0	0	0	0	1	0	0	1	2	1	1	0
	0	0	2	0	0	0	0	0	0	2	7	0	6	1
	0	0	0	0	2	0	2	0	2	0	0	0	2	0
	8	0	12	0	8	0	14	2	2	0	0	0	9	2
	0	0	2	0	1	0	2	0	1	1	1	1	2	0
	7	0	2	0	2	0	2	0	5	2	2	0	8	2
	0	0	0	0	2	0	2	0	3	0	2	0	4	0
	12	2	12	0	2	0	6	0	2	2	2	0	6	1
	2	1	2	1	1	1	2	1	2	1	0	1	2	1
	2	0	0	0	0	0	2	0	2	2	2	0	4	0
	1	0	2	0	1	0	1	0	1	0	1	0	XX	XX
	8	3	8	2	5	1	9	2	4	0	3	0	XX	XX
	1	0	1	0	1	0	1	0	1	1	1	1	XX	XX
	2	1	3	1	1	0	3	1	2	1	4	0	XX	XX

5A = Log maximum difference signal to noise, negative Z values, 300–500 ms
5B = Log maximum difference signal to noise, negative Z values, 0–500 ms
Total = Square root of sum of squares across features within an item
All = Square root of the sum of squares for a feature across items
Group I = Normal 1 (test), n = 62; chance level, 12
Group II = Learning disabled children, n = 56; chance level, 9
Group III = Normal 2 (control), n = 122, chance level, 23
Group IV = Specific learning disabled children, n = 49, chance level, 11

TABLE 29. Significance of Differences between Groups for the Distributions Shown in Table 28

Comparisons	Item 31												Item 62												Item 63											
	6	1A	1B	2A	2B	3A	3B	4A	4B	5A	5B	Total	6	1A	1B	2A	2B	3A	3B	4A	4B	5A	5B	Total	6	1A	1B	2A	2B	3A	3B	4A	4B	5A	5B	Total
I v II	3	2		2					2			3	3	3		2	3							3	3	3		2						1		3
I v III	3											3	3	1										3		1	3	3							3
I v IV									1			3	3											3	3	1	1									3
II v III	3	3		3	3			1				2	2	3		3	1							2	3	3	3	2		1			1			3
II v IV												3	3	3		2	2							3	3	2										3
III v IV	3	2							2			3	3											3	3	3	3	3	2						1	2

Note: See table 28 for definition of groups, items, and distributions.

1 = .05
2 = .01
3 = .001

Table 29—*Continued*

Item 64

Comparisons	6	1A	1B	2A	2B	3A	3B	4A	4B	5A	5B	Total
I v II	2	1	1			2	1		2			3
I v III	1				2							
I v IV	3		2									3
II v III	3	2	3		1	3	3		3			2
II v IV						2	1		1			2
III v IV	3		3			3						

Item 75

Comparisons	6	1A	1B	2A	2B	3A	3B	4A	4B	5A	5B	Total
I v II	3						1	1	1			3
I v III	2											
I v IV	3	1			2							1
II v III	3	1				2	1	1	3			1
II v IV									1			
III v IV	3	3			3	1						1

Item 76

Comparisons	6	1A	1B	2A	2B	3A	3B	4A	4B	5A	5B	Total
I v II						2	3					2
I v III	3		2									
I v IV	3											
II v III	3	1				1						
II v IV						1	1					1
III v IV	3	3				1						

All Items

Comparisons	6	1A	1B	2A	2B	3A	3B	4A	4B	5A	5B	Total
I v II	3	3		3		3	3	3				2
I v III	1	1	1	2	1							
I v IV	3	3		2	2				3			
II v III	3	3		3	3	3	3	3	3	1		
II v IV	2					3	2	2	3			
III v IV	3	3		3	3	3		1				1

TABLE 30. Distribution of Hits on Different EEG and EP Features, Alone and in Combination, for Groups of N and LD Children, in Percentage

	Group I	Group II	Group III	Group IV
Total EEG hits	8.0%	45.9	12.3	44.6
Only hit by EEG	8.0	12.6	12.3	26.8
Only spectral estimators	1.6	4.2	4.1	10.7
Only coherence	3.2	4.2	6.6	12.5
Both	3.2	4.2	1.6	3.6
Total EP hits	11.3	64.6	3.2	35.7
Only EP hits	11.3	31.2	3.2	17.8
Only EP features	0.0	12.5	2.4	1.8
Only Mahalanobis distance	8.1	8.3	0.8	7.1
Both	3.2	10.4	0.0	8.9
Both EEG and EP hits	0.0	33.3	0.0	17.9
Total hits any measure	19.4	77.1	15.5	62.5
None	80.6	22.9	84.5	37.5

References

Ahn, H.; Prichep, L.; John, E. R.; Baird, H.; Treptin, M.; and Kaye, H. 1980. "Developmental Equations Reflect Brain Dysfunctions." *Science* 210:1259–62.

Alvarez, A.; Pascual, R.; and Valdes, P. 1987. "U.S. EEG Developmental Equations Confirmed for Cuban Schoolchildren." *Electroencephalography and Clinical Neurophysiology* 67:330–32.

Barlow, J. S.; Morrell, L.; and Morrell, F. 1967. "Some Observations on Evoked Responses in Relation to Temporal Conditioning to Paired Stimuli in Man." *Proceedings of the International Colloquium on Mechanisms of Orienting Reactions in Man.* Czechoslovakia: Slovak Academy of Science.

Barnet, A. 1972. "Sensory Evoked Response Recording." In *Handbook of Electrophysiology and Clinical Electrophysiology,* edited by A. Remond. Amsterdam: Elsevier.

Barnet, A., and Goodwin, R. S. 1965. "Averaged Evoked Electroencephalographic Responses to Clicks in the Human Newborn." *Electroencephalography and Clinical Neurophysiology* 26:371–80.

Barnet, A., and Lodge, A. 1966. "Diagnosis of Deafness in Infants with the Use of Computer-Averaged Electroencephalographic Responses to Sound." *Journal of Pediatrics* 69:753–58.

———. 1967. "Click Evoked EEG Responses in Normal and Developmentally Retarded Infants. *Nature* 214:252–55.

Barnet, A.; Ohlrich, E. S.; and Shanks, B. L. 1971. "EEG Evoked Responses to Repetitive Auditory Stimulation in Normal and Down's Syndrome Infants." *Developmental Medicine and Child Neurology* 3:321–29.

Bartlett, F., and John, E. R. 1973. "Equipotentiality Quantified: The Anatomical Distribution of the Engram." *Science* 181:764–67.

Benton, A. L., and Bird, G. W. 1963. "The EEG and Reading Disability." *American Journal of Orthopsychiatry* 33:520–31.

Bigum, H. B.; Dustman, R. E.; and Beck, E. C. 1970. "Visual and Somatosensory Evoked Responses from Mongoloid and Abnormal

Children." *Electroencephalography and Clinical Neurophysiology* 28:576–85.

Birch, H. G. 1964. *Brain Damage in Children*. Baltimore: Williams and Wilkens.

Brown, W.; Marsh, J.; and Smith, J. 1973. "Contextual Meaning Effects on Speech-evoked Potentials." *Behavioral Biology* 9:755–61.

———. 1976. "Evoked Potential Waveform Differences Produced by the Perception of Different Meanings of an Ambiguous Phrase." *Electroencephalography and Clinical Neurophysiology* 41:113–23.

Buchsbaum, M., and Fedio, P. 1969. "Visual Information and Evoked Responses from the Left and Right Hemispheres. *Electroencephalography and Clinical Neurophysiology* 26:266–72.

———. 1970. "Hemispheric Differences in Evoked Potentials to Verbal and Nonverbal Stimuli in the Left and Right Fields." *Physiology and Behavior* 5:207–10.

Buchsbaum, M., and Wender, P. 1973. "Average Evoked Responses in Normal and Minimally Brain Dysfunctioned Children Treated with Amphetamine." *Archives in General Psychiatry* 29:764.

Callaway, E.; Tueting, P.; and Koslow, S., eds. 1978. *Event Related Potentials in Man*. New York: Academic Press.

Capute, A. J.; Niedermeyer, E. F.; and Richardson, F. 1968. "The Electroencephalogram in Children with Minimal Cerebral Dysfunction." *Pediatrics* 41:1104–14.

Clark, G. M. 1968. "A Summary of the Literature in Brain Damaged Children." In *Brain Damage in School Children,* edited by C. Haywood. Washington, D.C.: Council for Exceptional Children.

Clynes, M.; Kohn, M.; and Gradijan, J. 1967. "Computer Recognition of the Brain's Visual Perception through Learning the Brain's Physiologic Language." *Institute of Electrical and Electronic Engineers International Conference Record* 9:125–47.

Cody, D. T., and Bickford, R. G. 1965. "Cortical Audiometry; an Objective Method of Evaluating Auditory Acuity in Man." *Proceedings of the Mayo Clinic* 40:273–87.

Cohen, J. 1980. "Cerebral Evoked Responses in Dyslexic Children." In *Motivation Motor and Sensory Processes of the Brain,* edited by H. H. Kornhuber and L. Deecke. Amsterdam: Elsevier.

Cohen, J., and Breslin, P. W. 1984. "Visual Evoked Responses in Dyslexic Children." *Annals of New York Academy of Sciences* 425:338–43.

Cohn, R., and Nardini, J. 1958. "The Correlation of Bilateral Occipital Slow Activity in the Human EEG and with Certain Disorders of Behavior." *American Journal of Psychiatry* 115:44–54.

Colon, E. J.; Notermans, S. L. H.; deWeerd, J. P. C., and Kap, J. 1979. "The Discriminating Role of EEG Power Spectra in Dyslexic Children." *Journal of Neurology* 221:257–62.

Conners, C. K. 1971. "Cortical Visual Evoked Responses in Children with Learning Disorders." *Psychophysiology* 7:418–28.

———. 1973. "Psychological Assessment of Children with Minimal Brain Dysfunction." *Annals of New York Academy of Sciences* 205:285–302.

Copenhaver, R. M., and Perry, N. M. 1964. "Factors Affecting Visually Evoked Cortical Potentials Such As Impaired Vision of Varying Etiology. *Investigations in Ophthalmology* 3:665–75.

Cracco, R. Q., and Bodis-Wollner, I., eds. 1986. *Evoked Potentials: Frontiers in Clinical Neuroscience.* Vol. 3. New York: Alan R. Liss.

Cruz, F. F. de la; Fox, B. H.; and Roberts, R. H. 1973. *Minimal Brain Dysfunction.* New York: New York Academy of Sciences.

Davis, H. 1965. "The Young Deaf Child: Identification and Management." *Acta Oto-laryngologia* (Stockholm) supp. no. 206.

———. 1968. Average Evoked Response EEG Audiometry in North America." *Acta Oto-laryngologia* (Stockholm) 65:79–85.

Davis, H.; Hirsch, S. K.; Shelnutt, J.; and Bowers, C. 1976. "Further Validation of Evoked Response Audiometry (ERA)." *Journal of Speech and Hearing Research* 10:717–32.

Desmedt, J., ed. 1977. *Visual Evoked Potentials in Man.* Oxford: Claredon Press.

Dolce, G., and Kunkel, H., eds. 1975. *GEAN Computerized EEG Analysis.* Stuttgart: Fischer Verlag.

Donchin, E., and Lindsley, D. B. 1969. *Average Evoked Potentials.* Washington, D.C.: NASN SP-191.

Donchin, E., and Smith, D. B. 1970. "The CNV and Late Positive Wave of the Average Evoked Potential." *Electroencephalography and Clinical Neurophysiology* 29:201–3.

Donchin, E.; Tueting, P.; Ritter, W.; Kutas, M.; and Heffley, E. 1975. "On the Independence of the CNV and the P300 Components of the Human Averaged Evoked Potential." *Electroencephalography and Clinical Neurophysiology* 38:449–61.

Duffy, F. H.; Denckla, M. B.; Bartels, P. H.; and Sandini, G. 1980. "Dyslexia: Regional Differences in Brain Electrical Activity by Topographic Mapping." *Annals of Neurology* 7:412–20.

Duffy, F. H., and Geschwind, N., eds. 1985. *Dyslexia: A Neuroscientific Approach to Clinical Evaluation.* Boston: Little, Brown and Co.

Duffy, F. H., and McAnulty, G. B. 1985. "Brain Electrical Activity

Mapping (BEAM): The Search for a physiological Signature of Dyslexia." In Duffy and Geschwind 1985.

Dunlop, C. W.; McLachlan, E. M.; Webster, W. R.; and Day, R. H. 1964. "Auditory Habituation in Cats As a Function of Stimulus Intensity." *Nature* 203:874–75.

Dustman, R. E., and Beck, E. C. 1969. "The Effects of Maturation and Aging on the Waveform of Visually Evoked Potentials." *Electroencephalography and Clinical Neurophysiology* 26:2–11.

Eason, R. G.; White, C. T.; and Bartlett, N. 1970. "Effects of Checkerboard Pattern Stimulations on Evoked Cortical Responses in Relation to Check Size and Visual Field." *Psychonomic Science* 2:113–15.

Eisenberg, L. 1966. "The Epidemiology of Reading Retardation and a Program of Preventive Intervention." In *The Disabled Reader: Education for the Dyslexic Child,* edited by J. Money. Baltimore: Johns Hopkins Press.

Ellingson, R. J. 1967a. "Methods of Recording Critical Evoked Responses in the Human Infant." In *Regional Development on the Brain in Early Life,* edited by A. Minkowski. Oxford: Blackwell.
———. 1967b. "The Study of Brain Electrical Activity in Infants." In *Advances in Child Development and Behavior.* Vol. 3. edited by L. P. Lipsitt and C. C. Spiker. London: Academic Press.

Endroczi, E.; Fekete, T.; Lissak, K.; and Osvath, D. 1968. "Electroencephalographic Studies of the Habitation in Humans." *Acta Physiology Academy of Science Hungaricae Tomus* 34:311–18.

Engel, R., and Young, N. B. 1969. "Calibrated Pure Tone Audiograms in Normal Neonates Based on Evoked Electroencephalographic Responses." *Neuropädiatrie* 1:149–60.

Fein, G.; Galin, D.; Johnstone, J.; Yingling, C. D.; Marcus, M.; and Kiersch, M. E. 1983. "EEG Power Spectra in Normal and Dyslexic Children. I. Reliability during Passive Conditions." *Electroencephalography and Clinical Neurophysiology* 55:399–405.

Fein, G.; Galin, D.; Yingling, C. D., Johnstone, J.; and Nelson, M. A. 1984. "EEG Spectra in 9–13 Year Old Boys are Stable Over 1–3 Years." *Electroencephalography and Clinical Neurophysiology* 58:517–18.

Fernandez-Guardiole, A.; Roldan, E.; Fanjul, L.; and Castells, C. 1961. "Role of the Pupillary Mechanism in the Process of Habituation of the Visual Pathways." *Electroencephalography and Clinical Neurophysiology* 13:564–76.

Fields, C. 1969. "Visual Stimuli and Evoked Responses in the Rat." *Science* 165:1377–79.

Fruhstorfer, H.; Soveri, P.; and Jarvilehto, T. 1970. "Short Term Habituation of the Auditory Evoked Response in Man." *Electroen-cephalography and Clinical Neurophysiology* 28:153–61.

Gallagher, J. J. 1973. "New Educational Treatment Models for Children with Minimal Brain Dysfunction." In Cruz, Fox, and Roberts 1973.

Gasser, T.; Bacher, P.; and Mocks, J. 1982. "Transformations toward the Normal Distributions of Broad Band Spectral Parameters of the EEG." *Electroencephalography and Clinical Neurophysiology* 53:119–24.

Gasser, T.; Mocks, J.; and Bacher, P. 1983. "Topographic Factor Analysis of the EEG with Applications to Development and to Mental Retardation." *Electroencephalography and Clinical Neurophysiology* 45:445–63.

Gasser, T.; Mocks, J.; Leonard, H. G.; Bacher, P.; and Verleger, R. 1983. "The EEG of Mildly Retarded Children: Developmental Classification and Topographic Aspects." *Electroencephalography and Clinical Neurophysiology* 55:131–44.

Gellis, S. S., and Kagan, B. M. 1970. *Current Pediatric Therapy*. Vol. 4. Philadelphia: Saunders.

Gergen, J.; Conant, L.; Hills, D.; and Daudle, J. 1965. Personal communication.

Giannitrapani, D. 1967. "Developing Concepts of Lateralization of Cerebral Functions." *Cortex* 3:353–70.

Gibbs, F. A., and Gibbs, E. L. 1950. *Atlas of Encephalography*. Vol. 1: *Methodology and Controls*. Cambridge, Mass.: Addison-Wesley.
———. 1964. *Atlas of Encephalography*. Vol 3: *Neurological and Psychological Disorders*. Cambridge, Mass.: Addison-Wesley.

Gittelman, R.; Mannuzza, S.; Shenker, R.; and Bonagura, N. 1985. "Hyperactive Boys Almost Grown Up." *Archives of General Psychiatry* 42:937–47.

Gray, D. B., and Kavanagh, J. F. 1985. *Biobehavioral Measures of Dyslexia*. Maryland: York Press.

Graziani, L. J., and Weitzman, E. D. 1972. "Sensory Evoked Responses in the Neonatal Period and Their Application. In Remond 1972.

Grinberg, J., and John, E. R. 1974. Unpublished results.

Hagne, I.; Persson, J.; Mabnusson, R.; and Petersen, I. 1973. "Spectral analysis via Fast Fourier Transform of Waking EEG in Normal Infants." In Kellaway and Petersen 1973.

Harmony, T. 1983. *Functional Neuroscience*. Vol. 3: *Neurometric Diagnosis of Neuropathology*. Hillsdale, N.Y.: Lawrence Erlbaum Associates.

————. 1988. "Psychological Assessment of Children with Neuro-psychological Disorders." In *Handbook of Child Clinical Neuro-psychology*, edited by Cecil Reynolds, New York: Plenum Press.

Harmony, T.; Alvarez, A.; Pascual, R.; Ramos, A.; Marosi, E.; Diaz de Leon, A.; Valdes, P.; and Becker, J. 1987. "EEG Maturation of Children with Different Economic and Social Characteristics." *International Journal of Neuroscience.* 131.

Harmony, T.; Otero, T.; Ricardo, J.; and Fernandez, G. 1973. "Polarity Coincidence Correlation Coefficient and Signal Energy Ratio of the Ongoing EEG Activity. I. Normative Data." *Brain Research* 61:133–40.

Harmony, T.; Valdes, P.; and John, E. R. 1974. Work carried out in collaboration at the National Scientific Research Center of Cuba, Havana. Unpublished.

Harmony, T.; Valdes, P.; John, E. R.; Easton, P.; Ahn, H. 1974. Unpublished. Cited in Thatcher and John 1977.

Harter, M. R. 1971. "Evoked Cortical Responses to Checkerboard Patterns: Effect of Check-Size As a Function of Retinal Eccentricity." *Vision Research* 10:1365–76.

Harter, M. R., and White, C. T. 1968. "Effects of Contour and Check-Size on Visually Evoked Cortical Potentials. *Vision Research* 8:701–11.

————. 1970. "Evoked Cortical Response to Checkerboard Patterns: Effect of Check-Size As a Function of Visual Acuity." *Electroencephalography and Clinical Neurophysiology* 28:48–54.

Hechtman, L.; Weiss, G.; and Perlman, I. 1984. "Hyperactives As Young Adults: Past and Current Substance Abuse and Antisocial Behavior." *American Journal of Orthopsychiatry* 54:415–25.

Hernandez-Peon, R.; Scherrer, H.; and Jouvet, M. 1956. "Modification of Electrical Activity in the Cochlear Nucleus during Attention in Unanaesthetised Cats. *Science* 123:331–32.

Herrington, R. N., and Schneidau, P. 1968. "The effects of Imagery of the Visual Evoked Response." *Experientia* 24:1136–37.

HEW National Advisory Committee on Dyslexia and Related Reading Disorders. 1969. *Reading Disorders in the United States.* Washington, D.C.: Department of Health, Education and Welfare.

Hudspeth, W., and Jones, G. B. 1971. Unpublished observations.

Hughes, J. R. 1968. "Electroencephalography and Learning." In *Progress in Learning Disabilities.* Vol. 1., edited by H. R. Myklebust. New York: Grune and Stratton.

Hughes, J. R. 1985. "Evaluation of Electrophysiological Studies on Dyslexia." In Gray and Kavanagh 1985.

Hughes, J., and Myklebust, H. 1966. Unpublished results.

Hughes, J., and Park, G. 1966. "EEG in dyslexic children." Unpublished results.

Jasper, H. H. 1958. "The Ten-Twenty System of the International Federation." *Electroencephalography and Clinical Neurophysiology* 10:371–75.

John, E. R. 1961. "Higher Nervous Functions: Brain Functions and Learning." *Annual Review of Physiology* 23:451–84.

———. 1963. "Neural Mechanisms of Decision Making." In *Information Storage and Neural Control,* edited by W. S. Fields and W. Abbot. Springfield: Thomas.

———. 1967a. "Brain Correlates of Learning: Electrophysiological Studies of Conditioning." In *The Neurosciences: A Study Program,* edited by G. C. Quarton, T. Melnechuk, and F. O. Schmitt. New York: Rockefeller University Press.

———. 1967b. *Mechanisms of Memory.* New York: Academic Press.

———. 1972. "Mathematical Identification of Brain States Caused by Drugs." *International Journal of Neurobiology* 15:273–347.

———. 1973. "Memory Mechanisms in Instrumental Responding." *Science* 181:685–86.

———. 1974. "Assessment of Acuity, Color Vision and Shape Perception by Statistical Evaluation of Evoked Potentials." *Annals of Ophthalmology* 6:55–64.

———. 1976. "A Model of Consciousness." In *Consciousness and Self Regulation: Advances in Research,* edited by G. E. Schwartz and D. Shapiro. Vol. 1. New York: Plenum Press.

———. 1977. *Functional Neuroscience.* Vol. 2: *Neurometrics: Clinical Applications of Quantitative Electrophysiology.* New Jersey: Lawrence Erlbaum Associates.

John, E. R.; Ahn, H.; Prichep, L.; Trepetin, M.; Brown, D.; and Kaye, H. 1980. "Developmental Equations for the Electroencephalogram." *Science* 210:1255–58.

John E. R.; Bartlett, F.; Shimokochi, M.; and Kleinman, D. 1973. "Neural Readout from Memory." *Journal of Neurophysiology* 36:893–924.

John, E. R.; Grastyan, E.; Harmony, T.; and Morrell, F. 1967. Unpublished observations at IBRO Conference on Recent Advances in Brain Research, Budapest.

John E. R.; Herrington, R. N.; and Sutton, S. 1967. "Effects of Visual Form on the Evoked Response." *Science* 155:1439–42.

John, E. R.; Karmel, B. Z.; Corning, W. C.; Easton, P.; Brown, D.; Ahn, H.; John, M.; Harmony, T.; Prichep, L.; Toro, A.; Gerson, I.; Bartlett, F.; Thatcher, R.; Kaye, H.; Valdes, P.; and Schwartz, E. 1977a. "Neurometrics." *Science* 196:1393–1410.

John, E. R.; Prichep, L.; Ahn, H.; Brown, D.; Easton, P.; Karmel, B.; Thatcher, R.; and Toro, A. 1977b. "Neurometrics: Quantitative Electrophysiological Measurement of Organic Brain Dysfunction in Children. In Shagass 1977.

———. 1978. "Neurometrics: Quantitative Electrophysiological Analysis for Diagnosis of Learning Disabilities and Other Brain Dysfunctions." In Otto 1978.

John, E. R.; Prichep, L.; Ahn, H.; Easton, P., Fridman, J.; and Kaye H. 1983. "Neurometric Evaluation of Cognitive Dysfunctions and Neurological Disorders in Children." *Progress in Neurobiology* 21:239–90.

John, E. R.; Prichep, L. S.; and Easton, P. 1987. "Normative Data Banks and Neurometrics: Basic Concepts, Methods and Results of Norm Construction. In *Handbook of Electroencephalography and Clinical Neurophysiology*. Vol. 1: *Methods of Analysis of Brain Electrical and Magnetic Signals,* edited by A. S. Gevins and A. Remond. Amsterdam: Elsevier.

John, E. R.; Prichep, L. S.; Fridman, J., and Easton, P. 1988. "Neurometrics: Computer-Assisted Differential Diagnosis of Brain Dysfunctions." *Science,* 239:162–69.

John, E. R.; Ruchkin, D. S.; and Sachs, E. 1967. "Electrophysiological Contributions to the Study of Memory." In *The Organization of Recall,* edited by D. P. Kimble. New York: New York Academy of Sciences.

John, E. R.; Ruchkin, D. D.; and Vidal, J. 1978. "Measurement of Event-related Potentials." In Callaway, Tueting, and Koslow 1978.

John, E. R., and Schwartz, E. L. 1978. The Neurophysiology of Information Processing and Cognition." *Annual Review of Psychology* 29:1–29.

Johnston, V. L., and Chesney, G. L. 1974. "Electrophysiology Correlates of Meaning." *Science* 186:944–46.

Keidel, W. D., and Spreng, M. 1965. "Audiometric Aspects and Multisensory Power Functions of Electronically Averaged Evoked Cortical Response in Man. *Acta Oto-Laryngologia* (Stockholm) 59:201–8.

———. 1970. "Recent Status Results and Problems of Objective Audiometry in Man. Parts I and II. *Journal Francaise d'Oto-Rhino Laryngologie* 19.

Kellaway, P., and Petersen, I., eds. 1973. *Automation of Clinical Electroencephalography.* New York: Raven Press.

Keogh, B. 1971. "Hyperactive and Learning Disorders: Review and Speculation." *Exceptional Child* 39:101–10.

Key, B. J. 1965. "Correlation of Behavior with Changes in Amplitude of Cortical Potentials Evoked during Habituation by Auditory Stimuli." *Nature* 207:441–42.

Kinsbourne, M. 1973. "Minimal Brain Dysfunctions As a Neurodevelopmental Lag." In Cruz, Fox, and Roberts 1973.

Kirk, R. 1972. "Perceptual Defect and Role Handicap: A Theory of the Etiology of Schizophrenia." In *Orthomolecular Psychiatry: Treatment of Schizophrenia,* edited by D. R. Hawkings and L. D. Pawling. San Francisco: W. H. Freeman.

Klinke, R.; Fruhstorfer, H.; and Finkenzeller, P. 1968. "Evoked Responses As a Function of External and Stored Information." *Electroencephalography and Clinical Neurophysiology* 26:216–19.

Klove, H. 1959. "Relationship of Differential Electroencephalographic Patterns to Distribution of Wechsler-Bellevue Score." *Neurology* 9:871–76.

Korn, G., and Korn, T. 1968. *Mathematical Handbook for Scientists and Engineers.* New York: McGraw-Hill.

Leiman, A. L., and Christian, C. N. 1973. "Electrophysiology Analyses of Learning and Memory." In *The Physiological Basis of Memory,* edited by J. A. Deutsch. New York: Academic Press.

Leisman, G., and Ashkenazi, M. 1980. "Aetiological Factors in Dyslexia IV. Cerebral Hemispheres Are Functionally Equivalent." *Neuroscience* 11:157–64.

Lelord, G.; Laffont, F.; Jusseaume, P.; and Stephant, J. L. 1973. "Comparative Study of Conditioning of Averaged Evoked Responses by Couping Sound and Light in Normal and Autistic Children." *Psychophysiology* 10:415–25.

Loiselle, D. L.; Stamm, J. S.; Maitinsky, S.; and Whipple, S. 1980. "Evoked Potential and Behavioral Signs of Attentive Dysfunctions in Hyperactive Boys." *Psychophysiology* 17:193–201.

Lovrich, D., and Stamm, J. S. 1983. "Event-related Potential and Behavioral Correlates of Attention in Reading Retardation." *Journal of Clinical Neuropsychology* 5:13–37.

Lubar, J. F.; Bianchini, K. J.; Calhoun, W. H.; Lambet, E. W.; Brody, Z. H.; and Shabsin, H. S. 1985. "Spectral Analysis of EEG Differences between Children with and without Learning Disabilities. *Journal of Learning Disorders* 18:403–8.

Lubar, J. F., and Deering, W. M. 1981. *Behavioral Approaches to Neurology.* New York: Academic Press.

McCandless, G. A. 1967. "Clinical Application of Evoked Response Audiometry." *Journal of Speech Research* 10:468–78.

Marsh, J. T., and Worden, F. G. 1964. "Auditory Potentials during

Acoustic Habituation: Cochlear Nucleus, Cerebellum and Auditory Cortex." *Electroencephalography and Clinical Neurophysiology* 17:685–92.

Matousek, M., and Petersen, I. 1973. "Frequency Analysis of the EEG in Normal Children and Adolescents." In Kellaway and Petersen 1973.

Menkes, M.; Rowe, J. S.; and Menkes, J. H. 1967. "A Twenty-five Year Follow-up Study on the Hyperkinetic Child with Minimal Brain Dysfunction. *Pediatrics* 39:393–99.

Minskoff, J. G. 1973. "Differential Approaches to Prevalence Estimates of Learning Disabilities." In Cruz, Fox, and Roberts 1973.

Morrell, F., and Jasper, H. H. 1956. "Electrographic Studies of the Formation of Temporary Connections in the Brain." *Electroencephalography and Clinical Neurophysiology* 8:201.

Morrell, F., and Morrell, L. 1965. "Computer Aided Analysis of Brain Electrical Activity." In *The Analysis of Central Nervous System and Cardiovascular Data Using Computer Methods,* edited by L. D. Proctor and W. R. Adey. Washington, D.C.: NASA.

Muehl, S.; Knott, J.; and Benton, A. 1965. "EEG Abnormality and Psychological Test Performance in Reading Disabilities." *Cortex* 1:434–40.

Myklebust, H. R., and Boshes, B. 1969. *Minimal Brain Damage in Children.* Washington D.C.: Final Report to U.S. Public Health Service, S.S. Department H.E.W.

O'Gorman, G. 1962. "Conference on the Psychiatric Care of Deaf Children." *Lancet* 2:985.

Olken, B. S., and Chiappa, K. H. 1988. "Short-term Variability in EEG Frequency Analysis." *Electroencephalography and Clinical Neurophysiology* 69:191–98.

Ollo, C., and Squires, N. 1986. "Event-related Potentials in Learning Disabilities." In Cracco and Bodis-Wollner 1986.

Otero, G.; Harmony, T.; and Ricardo, J. 1975a. "Polarity Coincidence Correlation Coefficient and Signal Energy Ratio of Ongoing EEG Activity. III. Cerebral Vascular Lesions." *Activitas Nervora Superior* 17:127–30.

———. 1975b. "La Sinetria del EEG como metodo diagnostico en las lesiones cerebrales." Paper presented at the symposium on Applications of Computation in the Study of the Nervous System, Havana, Cuba, October 1975.

Otto, D., ed. 1978. *Multidisciplinary Perspectives in Event-related Brain Potential Research.* Washington, D.C.: U.S. Government Printing Office.

Otto, D.; Karrer, R.; Halliday, R.; Horst, R. L.; Klorman, R.; Squires, N.; Thatcher, R. W.; Fenelon, B.; and Lelord, G. 1984. "Developmental Aspects of Event-related potentials. Aberrant Development." *Annals of New York Academy of Science* 425:319–37.

Pavy, R., and Metcalfe, J. 1965. "The Abnormal EEG in Childhood Communication and Behavior Abnormalities." *Electroencephalography and Clinical Neurophysiology* 19:414.

Perry, N. W., Jr., and Childers, D. G. 1969. *The Human Visual Evoked Response: Method and Theory.* Springfield: Charles C. Thomas.

Posner, M. I.; Klein, R.; Summers, J.; and Buggie, S. 1973. On the Selection of Signals." *Memory and Cognition* 1:2–12.

Preston, M. S.; Guthrie, J. T.; and Childs, B. 1974. "Visual Evoked Responses (VERs) in Normal and Disabled Readers." *Psychophysiology* 11:452–57.

Pribram, K. H.; Spinelli, D. N.; and Kamback, M. C. 1967. "Electrocortical Correlates of Stimulus Response and Reinforcement." *Science* 157:94–95.

Prichep, L.; Gomez-Mont, F.; John, E. R.; and Ferris, S. H. 1983. "Neurometric Electroencephalographic Characteristics of Dementia." In *Alzheimer's Disease. The Standard Reference,* edited by B. Reisberg. New York: Free Press.

Prichep L.; Sutton, S.; and Hakerem, G. 1976. "Attention and the Auditory Evoked Potential in Hyperkinetic Children Treated with Methylphenidate and in Normal Children." *Psychophysiology* 13:419–28.

Ramos, A.; Schwartz, E.; and John, E. R. 1976. "Stable and Plastic Unit Discharge Patterns during Behavioral Generalization." *Science* 192:393–96.

Rapin, I., and Graziani, L. J. 1967. "Auditory Evoked Responses in Normal, Brain Damaged and Deaf Infants." *Neurology* (Minnesota) 17:881–94.

Rapin, I.; Ruben, R. J.; and Lyttle, M. 1970. "Diagnosis of Hearing Loss in Infants Using Auditory Evoked Responses." Paper presented to American Laryngology, Rhinology and Otolaryngology Society (Eastern), Boston.

Regan, D. 1972. *Evoked Potentials in Psychology, Sensory Physiology and Clinical Medicine.* New York: Wiley-Interscience.

Remond, A. 1972. *Handbook of Electroencephalography and Clinical Neurophysiology.* Vol. 15B. Amsterdam: Elsevier.

Rhodes L. E.; Dustman, R. E.; and Beck, E. C. 1969. "Visually Evoked Potentials of Bright and Dull Children." *Electroencephalography and Clinical Neurophysiology* 26:237.

Richlin, M.; Weisinger, M.; Weinstein, S.; Giannini, M.; and Morhen-
  stern, M. 1971. "Interhemispheric Asymmetries of Evoked Cortical
  Responses in Retarded and Normal Children." *Cortex* 7:98–105.
Ritvo, E. R.; Ornitz, E. M.; Walter, R. D.; and Haley, J. 1970. "Corre-
  lation of Psychiatric Diagnoses and EEG Findings: A Double-blind
  Study of 184 Hospitalized Children." *American Journal of Psychia-
  try* 126:988–96.
Rose, G. H., and Ellingson, R. J. 1970. "Ontogenesis of Evoked Poten-
  tials." In *Developmental Neurobiology,* edited by W. A. Himwich.
  Springfield: Charles C. Thomas.
Rouke, B. P. 1985. *Learning Disabilities in Children: Advances in
  Subtypal Analysis.* New York: Guilford Press.
Ruchkin, D. S., and John, E. R. 1966. "Evoked Potential Correlates of
  Generalization." *Science* 153:209–11.
Ruchkin, D. S., and Sutton, S. 1973. "Visual Evoked and Emitted
  Potentials and Stimulus Significance." *Bulletin of the Psychonom-
  ical Society* 2:144–46.
Ryers, F. W. 1967. "The Incidence of the EEG Abnormalities in a
  Dyslexic and a Control Group." *Journal of Clinical Psychology*
  23:334–36.
Satterfield, J. H. 1973. "EEG Issues in Children with Minimal Brain
  Dysfunction." In *Minimal Cerebral Dysfunction in Children,* edited
  by S. Walzer and P. H. Wolff. New York: Grune and Stratton.
Satterfield, J. H.; Hoppe, C. M.; and Schell, A. M. 1982. "A Prospec-
  tive Study of Delinquency in 110 Adolescent Boys with ADD and
  88 Normal Adolescent Boys." *American Journal of Psychiatry*
  139:795–98.
Satz, P.; Morris, R.; and Fletcher, M. 1985. "Hypotheses, Subtypes,
  and Individual Differences in Dyslexia: Some Reflections." In Gray
  and Kavanagh 1985.
Schenkenberg, T., and Dustman, R. E. 1970. "Visual, Auditory and
  Somatosensory Evoked Response Changes Related to Age, Hemi-
  sphere and Sex." *Proceedings of seventy-eighth Annual Convention
  of the American Psychological Association.*
Shagass, C., ed. 1977. *Psychopathology and Brain Dysfunction.* New
  York: Raven Press.
Sharpless, S., and Jasper, H. 1956. "Habituation of the Arousal Reac-
  tion." *Brain* 79:655–80.
Shelburne, S. A., Jr. 1972. "Visual Evoked Responses to Word and
  Nonsense Syllable Stimuli." *Electroencephalography and Clinical
  Neurophysiology* 32:17–25.
Shucard, D. W.; Cummins, K. R.; Gay, E.; Lairsmith; and Welanko,

P. 1985. "Electrophysiological Studies of Reading-disabled Children: In Search of Subtypes." In Gray and Kavanagh 1985.

Silverman, L. J., and Metz, A. S. 1973. "Numbers of Pupils with Specific Learning Disabilities in Local Public School in the United States: Spring 1970." In Cruz, Fox, and Roberts 1973.

Sklar, B.; Hanley, J.; and Simmons, W. W. 1972. "An EEG Experiment Aimed Toward Identifying Dyslexic Children." *Nature* 241:414–16.

————. 1973. "A Computer Analysis of EEG Spectral Signatures from Normal and Dyslexic Children." *IEEE Trans. Bio. Eng.* BME 20:20–26.

Sobotka, K. R., and May, J. G. 1977. "Visual Evoked Potentials and Reaction Time in Normal and Dyslexic Children." *Psychophysiology* 14:18–42.

Sokal, R. R., and Sneath, P. H. 1963. *Principles of Numerical Taxonomy.* San Francisco: W. H. Freeman.

Stevens, J. R.; Sachdev, K.; and Milstein, V. 1968. "Behavioral Disorders of Childhood and the Electroencephalogram." *Archives of Neurology* 18:160.

Sutton, S.; Braren, M.; Zubin, J.; and John E. R. 1965. "Evoked Potential Correlates of Stimulus Uncertainty." *Science* 150:1187–88.

Sutton, S.; Tueting, P.; Zubin, J.; and John, E. R. 1967. "Information Delivery and Sensory Evoked Potential." *Science* 155:1436–39.

Sutton, J. P.; Whitton, J. L.; Topa, M.; and Moldofsky, H. 1986. "Evoked Potential Maps in Learning Disabled Children." *Electroencephalography and Clinical Neurophysiology* 65:399–404.

Thatcher, R. W., and John, E. R. 1977. *Functional Neuroscience.* Vol. 1: *Foundations of Cognitive Processes.* New Jersey: Lawrence Earlbaum Associates.

Tizard, B. 1968. "Habituation of EEG and Skin Potential Changes in Normal and Severely Subnormal Children." *American Journal of Mental Deficiency* 73:34–40.

Torres, F., and Ayers, F. W. 1968. "Evaluation of EEG of Dyslexic Children." *Electroencephalography and Clinical Neurophysiology* 24:287.

Van Dis, H.; Corner, M.; Dapper, R.; and Hanewald, G. 1977. "Consistency of Individual Differences in the Human EEG during Wakefulness." *Electroencephalography and Clinical Neurophysiology* 43:574.

Vella, E. J.; Butler, S. R.; and Glass, A. 1972. "Electrical Correlate of Right Hemisphere Function." *Nature* 236:125–26.

Walter, W. Grey. 1963. "Specific and Non-Specific Responses and

Autonomic Mechanisms in Human Subjects during Conditioning."
Progress in Brain Research 1:395–401.

Walter, W. Grey; Cooper, R.; Aldridge, V. J.; McCallum, W. C.; and Winter, A. L. 1964. "Contingent Negative Variation: An Electric Sign of Sensorimotor Association and Expectancy in the Human Brain." *Nature* 203:380–84.

Weinberg, H.; Walter, W. Grey; and Crow, H. H. 1970. "Intracerebral Events in Humans Related to Real and Imaginary Stimuli." *Electroencephalography and Clinical Neurophysiology* 29:1–9.

Weiss, G., and Minde, K. K. 1974. "Follow-up Studies of Children Who Persist with Symptoms of Hyperactivity." In *Clinical Use of Stimulant Drugs in Children,* edited by C. K. Conners. New York: American Elsevier.

Weiss, G.; Minde, K. K.; Douglas, V.; Werry, J.; and Sykes, D. 1971. "Comparison of the Effects of Chlorpromazine, Dextroamphetamine Methylphenidate on the Behavior and the Functioning of Hyperactive Children. *Canadian Medical Association Journal* 104:20.

Wender, P. H. 1971. *Minimal Brain Dysfunction in Children.* New York: Wiley-Interscience.

Wikler, A.; Dixon, J. F.; and Parker, J. B., Jr. 1970. "Brain Function in Problem Children and Controls: Psychometric, Neurological and Electroencephalographic Comparisons." *American Journal of Psychiatry* 127:634–45.

Yingling, C. D.; Galin, D.; Fein, G.; Peltzman, D.; and Davenport, L. 1986. "Neurometrics Does Not Detect 'Pure' Dyslexic." *Electroencephalography and Clinical Neurophysiology* 63:426–30.

Authors

Dr. John and his co-authors were all part of the Brain Research Laboratories, Department of Psychiatry at New York University Medical Center when this book was written. Their present titles and affiliations are:

Dr. John is Professor of Psychiatry, Director of Brain Research Laboratories at New York University Medical Center, New York, New York 10016.

Dr. Prichep is Research Associate Professor, Department of Psychiatry, New York University Medical Center, New York, New York 10016.

Dr. Ahn is Professor of Psychology, Ajou University, Suwon, Korea.

Dr. Kaye is Associate Professor of Psychology, State University at Stony Brook, New York, 11794.

Mr. Brown is a data analyst consultant to the Brain Research Laboratories.

Dr. Easton is Research Assistant Professor, Department of Psychiatry, New York University Medical Center, New York, New York 10016.

Dr. Karmel is Associate Professor of Pediatrics and Psychiatry, Mt. Sinai Medical Center, New York, New York 10029.

Mr. Toro is Research Scientist in the Visual Science Division, Department of Psychiatry, New York University Medical Center, New York, New York 10016.

Dr. Thatcher is Professor and Director, Applied Neuroscience Institute, University of Maryland Eastern Shore, Princess Anne, Maryland.

Please address all correspondence to:

Dr. E. Roy John
Brain Research Laboratories
New York University Medical Center
550 First Avenue
New York, New York 10016

International Academy for Research In Learning Disabilities Monograph Series